WORK

A

Focus on Grammar

An **INTERMEDIATE** Course for Reference and Practice

SECOND EDITION

Marjorie Fuchs

Longman

FOCUS ON GRAMMAR: AN **INTERMEDIATE** COURSE FOR REFERENCE AND PRACTICE
Workbook

Pearson Education, 10 Bank Street, White Plains, NY 10606

Editorial director: Allen Ascher
Executive editor: Louisa Hellegers
Director of design and production: Rhea Banker
Development editors: Angela Malovich Castro and Bill Preston
Production manager: Alana Zdinak
Managing editor: Linda Moser
Senior production editor: Virginia Bernard
Production editor: Christine Lauricella
Senior manufacturing manager: Patrice Fraccio
Manufacturing manager: David Dickey
Cover design: Rhea Banker
Text design adaptation: Rainbow Graphics
Text composition: Rainbow Graphics
Photo credits: **p. 4** Rubberball Productions; **p. 14** AP/Wide World Photos; **p. 15** Library of Congress; **p. 17** AP/Wide World Photos; **p. 54** AP/Wide World Photos; **p. 74** Allsport Photography (USA), Inc; **p. 74** AP/Wide World Photos; **p. 87** Rubberball Productions; **p. 91** Hulton Getty

0–201–34678–8

5 6 7 8 9 10—BAH—04 03 02

CONTENTS

ABOUT THE AUTHOR

Marjorie Fuchs has taught ESL at New York City Technical College and LaGuardia Community College of the City University of New York and EFL at the Sprach Studio Lingua Nova in Munich, Germany. She holds a Master's Degree in Applied English Linguistics and a certificate in TESOL from the University of Wisconsin–Madison. She has authored or co-authored many widely used ESL textbooks, notably *On Your Way: Building Basic Skills in English, Crossroads, Top Twenty ESL Word Games, Around the World: Pictures for Practice, Families: Ten Card Games for Language Learners, Focus on Grammar: A High-Intermediate Course for Reference and Practice,* and the *Workbooks* to the *Longman Dictionary of American English,* the *Longman Photo Dictionary, The Oxford Picture Dictionary,* and the *Vistas* series.

UNIT

PRESENT PROGRESSIVE AND SIMPLE PRESENT TENSE

 SPELLING

Add **-ing** *to these verbs to form the present participle. Add* **-s** *or* **-es** *to form the third-person-singular form. Make spelling changes where necessary.*

	-ing	**-s or -es**
1. start	starting	starts
2. get	_____	_____
3. try	_____	_____
4. plan	_____	_____
5. have	_____	_____
6. do	_____	_____
7. match	_____	_____
8. grab	_____	_____
9. give	_____	_____
10. say	_____	_____

2 SIMPLE PRESENT TENSE OR PRESENT PROGRESSIVE

Complete the sentences about a student, Antonio Lopes. Use the correct form of the verbs in parentheses ( ).

1. It's 8:00 A.M. Antonio Lopes _____ is driving _____ to school.
      (drive)

2. He _____ to school every day.
              (drive)

3. The trip usually _____ 25 minutes.
                        (take)

4. Today it _____ 25 minutes.
              (not take)

5. It _____ much longer.
         (take)

(continued on next page)

1

6. Workers _____ the highway this morning.
   (repair)

7. Because of the construction, Antonio _____ Parson Road.
   (use)

8. He _____ usually _____ Parson
   (not use)
   Road.

9. Normally, he _____ Route 93.
   (take)

10. Traffic always _____ faster on Route 93.
    (move)

11. Today, the weather _____ the traffic, too.
    (slow down)

12. It _____ hard, and the roads are slippery.
    (rain)

13. Antonio _____ to drive in the rain.
    (not like)

14. Antonio's a careful driver, and he always _____ slowly
    (drive)
    when the roads are wet.

15. The radio is on, and Antonio _____ to the traffic report.
    (listen)

16. He always _____ to the radio on his way to work.
    (listen)

17. The announcer _____ an accident on Parson Road.
    (describe)

18. Antonio _____ to be late for school, but there's nothing he
    (not want)
    can do.

19. Traffic _____ because of the accident.
    (not move)

20. Antonio _____ to drive when the traffic is bad.
    (hate)

21. He never _____ relaxed when he is behind the wheel.
    (feel)

22. He _____ he can't do anything about the traffic conditions.
    (know)

23. Antonio _____ he were on the bus instead.
    (wish)

❸ PERSONALIZATION

Complete these statements with information about yourself. Use the present progressive or the simple present tense.

1. At the moment _____.

2. I always _____.

3. I sometimes _____, but now I _____.

4 PRESENT PROGRESSIVE OR SIMPLE PRESENT TENSE

Read and complete these postcards with the present progressive or simple present tense form of the verbs in the boxes.

blow	build	feel	fly	know	shine	~~sit~~

1.

Dear Megan,

Hi! I _____'m sitting_____ on the beach at Ipanema. The weather is beautiful.
       1.

The sun _____, and there isn't a cloud in the sky. A soft breeze
      2.

_____ . It _____ great.
     3.   **4.**

Some beautiful tropical birds (you _____ the kind)
          5.

_____ above. Children _____
     6.   **7.**

sand castles. This is the place to be!

           Wish you were here,

           Ashley

get	have	look	stand	start	take	travel

2.

Dear Carlos,

Ana and I _____ through England. Right now I _____ in front
     1.   **2.**

of Buckingham Palace. It's a cloudy day. The sky _____ darker by the minute. It
          3.

_____ like it's going to rain. Ana _____ her camera, and she
   4.   **5.**

_____ pictures. Oh, no! It _____ to rain.
   6.   **7.**

See you in a few weeks!

Marcos

(continued on next page)

| help | improve | live | miss | speak | study | want |

3.

Dear Amanda,

Here I am in Paris! I _____ French and

_____ with a French family—the Michauds. My French

2.

_____ because I always _____ it

3.   4.

"at home."

The Michauds are great. They _____ me find a job.

5.

I _____ to save enough money to travel in August. Why

6.

don't you come and visit me? I _____ you!

7.

Melissa

5 AFFIRMATIVE STATEMENTS

Mario and Silvia are students. Look at what they do every day. Write sentences about their activities. Choose between the present progressive and the simple present tense.

Mario

A.M.
7:30 get up
8:00 watch TV
8:30 go to school

P.M.
12:00 have lunch
3:00 study at the library
4:00 go home
5:00 do homework
6:00 have dinner
7:00 play computer games
8:00 read the newspaper

Silvia

A.M.
7:30 get up
8:00 listen to the radio
8:30 go to school

P.M.
12:00 have lunch
3:00 play basketball
4:00 visit her grandmother
5:00 do homework
6:00 practice the guitar
7:00 make dinner
8:00 wash the dishes

1. At 7:30 A.M., <u>Mario and Silvia get up.</u>

2. It's 8:00 A.M. <u>Mario is watching TV. Silvia is listening to the radio.</u>

3. At 8:30 A.M., _____

4. It's noon. _____

5. At 3:00 P.M., _____

6. At 4:00 P.M., _____

7. It's 5:00 P.M. _____

8. At 6:00 P.M., _____

9. At 7:00 P.M., _____

10. It's 8:00 P.M. _____

6 AFFIRMATIVE AND NEGATIVE STATEMENTS

Read this letter from Mario. Mario made five mistakes in facts. Look at his schedule in Exercise 5. Then correct Mario's mistakes.

> Dear Carlo,
>
> ○ How are you? I'm really busy, so this is going to be a short letter. I get up at 7:00 every day. Then I listen to the radio for half an hour. (It helps my English comprehension.) After that, Silvia and I go to school. My classes are good. I'll tell you more about them in my next letter. Silvia and I have lunch together at noon. After classes, I study at the library. I go home at 4:00, but Silvia visits <u>her</u> grandfather.
>
> It's now 6:30. Silvia is practicing the piano. I usually have dinner at this time, but tonight I'm going to eat with Silvia. She doesn't make dinner until 7:00.
>
> ○ After dinner, I usually play computer games. Then I watch the news at 8:00. And that's my day!
>
> Let me know how you are.
>
> Mario

1. <u>He doesn't get up at 7:00.</u>

<u>He gets up at 7:30.</u>

(continued on next page)

2. _____

_____

3. _____

_____

4. _____

_____

5. _____

_____

7 YES/NO QUESTIONS AND SHORT ANSWERS

Look at the schedules in Exercise 5. Ask and answer the questions.

1. (Mario and Silvia / go to school?)

A: _Do Mario and Silvia go to school?_

B: _Yes, they do._

2. (When / Mario and Silvia / get up?)

A: _____

B: _____

3. (Silvia / watch TV in the morning?)

A: _____

B: _____

4. It's 12:00. (What / they / do / now?)

A: _____

B: _____

5. It's 2:00. (Mario / study at the library now?)

A: _____

B: _____

6. (he / do his homework at school?)

A: _____

B: _____

7. (When / Silvia / play basketball?)

    A: _____

    B: _____

8. (Mario / play computer games before dinner?)

    A: _____

    B: _____

8 ADVERBS AND WORD ORDER

Put these words in the correct order to form statements. Use the correct form of the verb in parentheses.

1. Mario / the newspaper / (read) / always

    _Mario always reads the newspaper._____

2. on time / usually / Silvia / (be)

    _____

3. never / school / Silvia and Mario / (miss)

    _____

4. these days / they / (study) / English

    _____

5. usually / they / Italian / (speak)

    _____

6. (speak) / English / now / they

    _____

7. (do) / their homework / Silvia and Mario / always

    _____

8. (be) / Mario / tired / often

    _____

9. usually / (eat) / the students / in school / lunch

    _____

(continued on next page)

10. hungry / they / (be) / always

_____

11. Silvia / at the moment / (have) / a snack

_____

12. (go) / to bed / rarely / Silvia / late

_____

9 EDITING

Read this student's letter. Find and correct twelve mistakes in the use of the simple present tense and present progressive. The first mistake is already corrected.

> Dear Andrew,
>
>   Hi, How are you? I ~~write~~ 'm writing you this letter on the bus. I hope you can read my writing. They
>
> do some repairs on the road, so it's bumpy and the bus shakes. Guess what? I am having a
>
> job as a clerk in the mail room of a small company. The pay isn't good, but I'm liking the
>
> people there. They're all friendly, and we are speaking Spanish all the time. I'm also taking
>
> Spanish classes at night at a language institute. The class is meeting three times a week. It just
>
> started last week, so I'm not knowing many of the other students yet. They seem nice, though.
>
>   I'm thinking that I'm beginning to get accustomed to living here. At first I experienced
>
> some "culture shock." I understand that this is quite normal. But these days I meet more and
>
> more people because of my job and my class, so I'm feeling more connected to things.
>
>   What do you do these days? Do you still look for a new job?
>
>   Please write when you can. I always like to hear from you.
>
>   Yours,
>
>   Brian

IMPERATIVE

① AFFIRMATIVE AND NEGATIVE IMPERATIVES

Complete the chart. Use the words in the box.

backward	in	l̶e̶f̶t̶	loudly	off	slowly	tight
down	late	light	low	shut	small	up

Affirmative	**Negative**
1. Bend your *right* leg.	<u> Don't bend your left leg. </u>
2. _____	Don't look *up*.
3. Lean *forward*.	_____
4. _____	Don't take a *big* step.
5. Breathe *out*.	_____
6. _____	Don't count *quickly*.
7. Speak *softly*.	_____
8. _____	Don't keep your eyes *open*.
9. Wear *loose* clothes.	_____
10. _____	Don't wear *heavy* clothes.
11. Turn the lights *on*.	_____
12. _____	Don't turn the music *down*.
13. _____	Don't put the heat on *high*.
14. Come *early*.	_____

2 AFFIRMATIVE AND NEGATIVE IMPERATIVES

Ada, a student, is asking her friends for directions to Jim's Gym. Look at the map and complete the conversation. Use the words in the box.

~~ask~~	continue	go	make	ride	~~take~~	walk
be	cross	have	pass	stop	turn	work

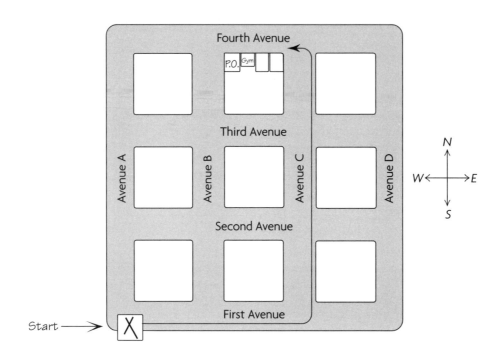

ADA: I'm going to take an exercise class at Jim's Gym. Do you know how to get there?

BOB: Jim's Gym? _____Ask_____ Chen. He's taking a class there.
   1.

ADA: I didn't know that. Which bus do you take to the gym, Chen?

CHEN: Oh, _____don't take_____ the bus! It's not far from here.
   2.
   _____ or _____ your bike.
   3.   **4.**
   It's good exercise!

ADA: I'll walk. How do I get there?

CHEN: _____ two blocks east on First Avenue.
   5.

ADA: East? You mean turn left?

CHEN: No. _____ left. Go right when you leave the building.
   6.
   OK? Then _____ a left turn when you get to Avenue C.
   7.

_____ on Avenue C, but _____
                                                8.   9.
when you reach Fourth Avenue. _____ Fourth Avenue.
                                                                                    10.
It's another left at Fourth. But _____ careful. Jim's Gym
                                                                        11.
is small and it's easy to miss. _____ the post office. The
                                                                          12.
gym is right before it.

ADA: Thanks.

CHEN: Sure. _____ fun! _____ too hard!
                                          13.   14.

❸ EDITING

Read Ada's note to her roommate. Find and correct five mistakes in the use of imperatives. The first mistake is already corrected.

Sara,

                     Call
Your mother called. ~~Calls~~ her at your sister's tonight.

Don't you call after 10:00, though.

I went to the gym.

Wash please the dishes and threw out the trash.

If anyone calls for me, takes a message.

                    Thanks a lot.
                    A.

❹ PERSONALIZATION

Draw a map and give directions to a place near you. Use your own paper.

SIMPLE PAST TENSE

---

1 SPELLING: REGULAR AND IRREGULAR VERBS

Write the simple past tense form of the verbs.

Base Form	Simple Past		Base Form	Simple Past
1. answer	answered		13. live	lived
2. buy	bought		14. meet	met
3. catch	catched		15. need	needed
4. do	did		16. open	opened
5. look	looked		17. put	put
6. find	found		18. read	read
7. give	gave		19. say	said
8. hurry	hurried		20. think	thought
9. see	saw		21. understand	understood
10. die	died		22. vote	voted
11. kiss	kissed		23. win	won
12. come	came		24. feel	felt

25. The past of *be* is ____was____ or ____were____.

---

2 AFFIRMATIVE AND NEGATIVE STATEMENTS: *BE*

*Look at the chart of famous writers of the past. Complete the sentences with **was**, **wasn't**, **were**, and **weren't**.*

Isaak Babel	1894-1941	Russia	short-story writer, playwright*
James Baldwin	1924-1987	United States	author, playwright
Honoré de Balzac	1799-1850	France	novelist
Simone de Beauvoir	1908-1966	France	novelist, essayist**
Giovanni Boccaccio	1313-1375	Italy	poet, storyteller
Karel Čapek	1890-1938	Czechoslovakia	novelist, essayist
Agatha Christie	1890-1976	England	mystery writer
Lorraine Hansberry	1930-1965	United States	playwright
Pablo Neruda	1904-1973	Chile	poet

*A *playwright* is a person who writes plays. **An *essayist* is a person who writes essays.

1. Simone de Beauvoir _____wasn't_____ a French poet. She _____was_____ a French novelist.
2. Giovanni Boccaccio _____was_____ born in 1313.
3. James Baldwin and Lorraine Hansberry _____weren't_____ American poets. They _____were_____ playwrights.
4. Karel Čapek _____wasn't_____ a poet.
5. Pablo Neruda _____was_____ from Chile.
6. Honoré de Balzac _____ a playwright. He _____was_____ a novelist.
7. Agatha Christie _____wasn't_____ American. She _____was_____ English.
8. Isaak Babel _____was_____ Russian. He _____wasn't_____ French.
9. Simone de Beauvoir and Honoré de Balzac _____were_____ both French.
10. Pablo Neruda and Simone de Beauvoir _____were_____ both born in the early 1900s.

3 QUESTIONS AND ANSWERS WITH THE PAST TENSE OF *BE*

Ask and answer questions about the people in Exercise 2. Use **was** *and* **wasn't**.

1. James Baldwin / a playwright?

   A: _Was James Baldwin a playwright?_

   B: _Yes, he was._

2. Where / Simone de Beauvoir from?

   A: where was Simone de Beauvoir from?

   B: He was france

3. What nationality / Pablo Neruda?

   A: what nationality was Pablo Neruda?

   B: He was Chilean

4. Who / Boccaccio?

   A: who was Boccaccio?

   B: He was a Italian poet

5. Agatha Christie / French?

   A: was A. ch. french?

   B: No, she was

6. What nationality / Lorraine Hansberry?

   A: what nationality was Lor. Hans

   B: She was American.

(continued on next page)

7. Honoré de Balzac / a poet?

A: <u>Was Honoré de Balzac a poet.</u>

B: _____

8. When / Karel Čapek / born?

A: <u>When was Karel Capek born?</u>

B: _____

9. Who / Isaak Babel?

A: <u>Who was Isaak Babel?</u>

B: <u>He was.</u>

4 AFFIRMATIVE STATEMENTS

Complete these short biographies. Use the simple past tense form of the verbs in the boxes.

| ~~be~~ die ~~include~~ ~~spend~~ translate ~~write~~ |

1. Lin Yutang (1895–1976) <u>was</u> a Chinese-American writer.
He <u>spend</u> most of his life in the United States. Dr. Lin
<u>wrote</u> a lot about his native China. His books
<u>included</u> several novels. He also <u>translated</u> other
people's works. Lin <u>died</u> at the age of 81.

| ~~be~~ begin call have ~~live~~ paint |

2. Anna Mary Robertson Moses (1860–1961) <u>was</u> an
American painter. She <u>lived</u> on a farm in New York State.
Because she <u>began</u> painting in her seventies, people
<u>called</u> her Grandma Moses. She never <u>had</u> any
formal art training. Moses <u>painted</u> simple, colorful scenes of
farm life.

be   build   ~~fly~~   last   ~~take place~~   ~~watch~~

3. Orville Wright (1871–1948) and **Wilbur Wright** (1867–1912)

__were__ American airplane inventors. The two brothers

__built__ their first planes in their bicycle shop in Ohio. On
2.

December 17, 1903, Orville __flew__ their plane, *Flyer 1*, a
3.

distance of 120 feet. Wilbur, four men, and a boy __watched__
4.

from the ground. This first controlled, power-driven flight

__took place__ near Kitty Hawk, North Carolina. It __lasted__
5.   6.

only about 12 seconds.

---

5 QUESTIONS AND ANSWERS

Ask and answer questions about the people in Exercise 4.

Biography 1

1. When / Lin Yutang / live?

  A: When did Lin Yutang live?

  B: He lived from 1895 to 1976.

2. What / he / do?

  A: What did he do?

  B: he

3. he / write poetry?

  A: Did he write poetry.

  B: No, he didn't

4. Where / he / spend most of his life?

  A: Where did he spend most of his life?

  B:

(continued on next page)

Biography 2

5. What / people / call Anna Mary Robertson Moses?

A: What did people can

B: th.

6. What / she / do?

A: What did she do?

B:

7. When / she / begin painting?

A: When did she begin painting?

B:

8. she / have formal art training?

A: Did she have formal art tran.

B:

Biography 3

9. Where / the Wright brothers / build their first planes?

A: Where did the wright brothers build

B:

10. both brothers / fly the *Flyer 1*?

A: Did both brothers fly t

B:

11. Where / first controlled flight / take place?

A: Where did the first controlled flight take place?

B:

12. How long / the flight / last?

A: How long did the flight last?

B:

6 NEGATIVE STATEMENTS

There were a lot of similarities between the Wright brothers. But there were also differences. Complete the chart about the differences between Orville and Wilbur.

Orville	Wilbur
1. Orville talked a lot.	Wilbur didn't talk a lot.
2. Orville didn't spend a lot of time alone.	Wilbur spent a lot of time alone.
3. Orville didn't have serious	Wilbur had serious health problems.
4. Orville grew a moustache.	Wilbur didn't have a moustache
5. Orville didn't lose	Wilbur lost most of his hair.
6. Orville took courses in Latin.	Wilbur didn't take course
7. Orville liked to play jokes.	Wilbur didn't like to pla.
8. Orville dressed very fashionably.	Wilbur didn't dress very fashionably
9. Orville played the guitar.	Willbur didn't play the guitar.
10. Orville didn't build	Wilbur built the first glider.
11. Orville didn't make	Wilbur made the first attempts to fly.
12. Orville didn't choose	Wilbur chose the location of Kitty Hawk.
13. Orville had a lot of patience.	~~Orved~~ Willbur didn't have
14. Orville lived a long life.	

7 EDITING

Read this student's short biography of a famous person. Find and correct six mistakes in the use of the simple past tense. The first mistake is already corrected.

Pablo Neruda *(1904–1973) Pablo Neruda* ~~were~~ was *a famous poet, political activist, and diplomat. He was born in Parral, Chile. When he was seventeen, he* ~~gone~~ went *to Santiago to continue his education. He did not* ~~finished~~ finish*, but he soon published his first book. Neruda* ~~spends~~ spent *the next several decades traveling and continuing to write poetry. In 1971, while he was Chile's ambassador to France, he* ~~winned~~ won *the Nobel Prize in literature. He* ~~dead~~ died *two years later.*

USED TO

1 AFFIRMATIVE STATEMENTS

Life in the United States isn't the way it used to be. Complete the chart.

	In the Past	**Now**
1.	_People used to ride_ horses.	People ride in cars.
2.	_____ by candlelight.	People read by electric light.
3.	_____ over open fires.	People cook in microwave ovens.
4.	_____ in propeller airplanes.	People fly in jet planes.
5.	_____ large families.	People have small families.
6.	_____ all of their clothes by hand.	People wash most of their clothes in washing machines.
7.	_____ manual typewriters.	People use word processors and computers.
8.	_____ twenty-five days to get a message from New York to San Francisco.	It takes just a few seconds.

2 AFFIRMATIVE AND NEGATIVE STATEMENTS

*Complete the sentences about the assistant manager of a California bank, Yoko Shimizu. Use **used to** or **didn't use to** and the verbs in parentheses ( ).*

1. Yoko _____*used to be*_____ a full-time student. Now she
      (be)
   has a job at a bank.

2. She _____ with a computer. Now she uses one

(work)

every day.

3. She _____ a car. Now she owns a 1999 Toyota Corolla.

(have)

4. Yoko _____ the bus to work. Now she drives.

(take)

5. The bus _____ crowded. These days it's hard to find a seat.

(be)

6. Yoko _____ in New York. Then she moved to Los Angeles.

(live)

7. She _____ Los Angeles. Now she thinks it's a nice city.

(like)

8. She _____ a lot of people in Los Angeles. Now she has a lot

(know)

of friends there.

9. She _____ to New York several times a year. These days she

(return)

doesn't go there very often.

10. She _____ a lot of letters. Now she makes a lot of phone

(write)

calls instead.

❸ QUESTIONS AND ANSWERS

*Look at these two ID cards. Ask and answer questions about Sara
Rogers, a new employee at City Savings Bank. Use **used to** and the cues
in parentheses ( ).*

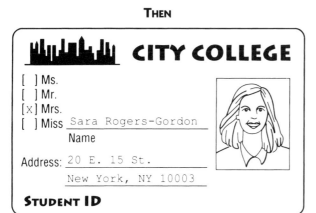

(continued on next page)

1. (live in California?)

   A: <u>   Did she use to live in California?   </u>

   B: <u>   No, she didn't.   </u>

2. Sara recently moved to Los Angeles. (Where / live?)

   A: _____

   B: _____

3. This is her first job. (What / do?)

   A: _____

   B: _____

4. Sara looks very different from before. She has short hair and wears glasses. (have long

   hair?)

   A: _____

   B: _____

5. (wear glasses?)

   A: _____

   B: _____

6. Sara's last name is different from before. (be married?)

   A: _____

   B: _____

7. (use *Ms.* before her name?)

   A: <u>Did she use to use Ms before Her name?</u>

   B: <u>No, she didn't</u>

4 EDITING

*Read this student's journal entry. Find and correct five mistakes in the
use of* **used to**. *The first mistake is already corrected.*

Journal

Sunday, Oct. 5

    Today I ran into an old classmate. At first, I almost didn't recognize him! He looked so

different. He used to ~~had~~ very dark hair. Now he's almost all gray. He also used to being a little
  (have)   *(be)*

heavy. Now he's quite thin. And he was wearing a suit and tie! I couldn't believe it. He never

used to dress that way. He only used to wear jeans! His personality seemed different, too. He

didn't used to talk very much. Now he seems very outgoing.

    I wonder what he thought about me! I'm sure I look and act a lot different from the way I

was used to, too!
  (be)

---

5 PERSONALIZATION

*Write five sentences about how your life used to be different from the
way it is now. Use* **used to**.

1. I used to go to parties every weekend,
2. now I don't.
3. I used to wear suit and Tie,
4. now I wear jeans, Tshirt, sneakers.
5. I used to go play football every weekend too,
   Now I go to work all time.

 PAST PROGRESSIVE AND SIMPLE PAST TENSE

Frank Cotter is a financial manager. Look at his schedule and complete the sentences.

	10 Wednesday
9:00–10:00	meet with Ms. Jacobs
10:00–11:00	write financial reports
11:00–12:00	answer correspondence
12:00–1:00	eat lunch with Mr. Webb at Sol's Cafe
1:00–3:00	attend lecture at City University
3:00–4:00	discuss budget with Alan
4:00–5:00	return phone calls

1. At 9:30 Mr. Cotter _____was meeting with_____ Ms. Jacobs.

2. At 9:30 he _____ financial reports.

3. At 11:30 he _____ correspondence.

4. At 12:30 he and Mr. Webb _____ lunch.

5. They _____ at Frank's Diner.

6. At 2:00 he _____ a lecture.

7. At 3:30 he and Alan _____ reports.

8. They _____ the budget.

9. At 4:30 he _____ correspondence.

10. He _____ phone calls.

② QUESTIONS AND ANSWERS WITH THE PAST PROGRESSIVE

Look at the schedule in Exercise 1. Ask questions and give short answers.

1. Mr. Cotter / meet / with Mr. Webb at 9:30?

    A: ___Was Mr. Cotter meeting with Mr. Webb at 9:30?___

    B: ___No, he wasn't.___

2. What / he / do at 9:30?

    A: _____

    B: _____

3. Mr. Cotter / write police reports at 10:30?

    A: _____

    B: _____

4. What kind of reports / he / write?

    A: _____

    B: _____

5. What / he / do at 11:30?

    A: _____

    B: _____

6. he / have lunch at 12:00?

    A: _____

    B: _____

7. Who / eat lunch with him?

    A: _____

    B: _____

(continued on next page)

8. Where / they / have lunch?

A: _____

B: _____

9. Who / he / talk to at 3:30?

A: _____

B: _____

10. What / they / discuss?

A: _____

B: _____

3 STATEMENTS WITH THE PAST PROGRESSIVE
AND SIMPLE PAST TENSE

Read about an explosion at the World Trade Center in New York City.
Complete the story with the past progressive or simple past tense form
of the verbs in parentheses ( ).

> On February 26, 1993, a bomb ___exploded___ in New York City's World
> **1. (explode)**
>
> Trade Center. At the time, 55,000 people ___were working___ in the Twin Towers,
> **2. (work)**
>
> and thousands of others ___were visiting___ the 110-story world-famous tourist
> **3. (visit)**
>
> attraction.
>
> The explosion, which ___took place___ a little after noon, ___killed___ six
> **4. (take place)** **5. (kill)**
>
> people and ___injured___ more than a thousand others. It ___took___ all
> **6. (injure)** **7. (take)**
>
> day and half the night to get everyone out of the building.
>
> When the bomb ___exploded___, the lights ___went out___, the elevators
> **8. (explode)** **9. (go out)**

___stopped___, and fires ___started___. Many people were in the wrong place
10. (stop)   11. (start)

at the wrong time. Four co-workers ___were eating___ lunch in their offices when
12. (eat)

the explosion ___shook___ the Twin Towers. When the blast ___occured___,
13. (shake)   14. (occur)

the building's walls ___crumbled___ and the ceilings ___collapsed___. Rescue
15. (crumble)   16. (collapse)

workers ___arrived___ within fifteen minutes and ___found___ the four
17. (arrive)   18. (find)

workers dead.

One man ___was walking___ in the garage beneath the World Trade Center when
19. (walk)

the bomb ___went off___. He ___had___ a heart attack while rescue
20. (go off)   21. (have)

workers ___were carrying___ him to the ambulance.
22. (carry)

Sixty schoolchildren were luckier. They ___were riding___ the huge elevators
23. (ride)

when the lights ___went out___ and the elevators ___stopped___. The children
24. (go out)   25. (stop)

and their teachers ___had to___ stand in the hot, dark space as they waited
26. (have to)

for help. Six hours later, when the elevator ___reached___ the ground floor, the
27. (reach)

school bus driver ___was waiting___ for them. He ___drove___ the children
28. (wait)   29. (drive)

home to their worried families. How did the children feel while all this

___happened___? "We were scared," they answered.
30. (happen)

This is one class trip they will never forget.

4 QUESTIONS WITH THE PAST PROGRESSIVE AND SIMPLE PAST TENSE

Reporters are interviewing people about the explosion at the World Trade Center. Use the past progressive and the simple past tense to write the interview questions.

1. What / you do / when you feel the explosion?

   A: What were you doing when you felt the explosion?

   B: I was sitting in my chair.

2. What happen / when the bomb explode?

   A: What happened when the bomb exploded?

   B: I flew off my chair and landed on the floor.

3. What / the schoolchildren do / when the lights go out?

   A: What were the school children doing when the lights went out?

   B: They were riding the elevator.

4. How many people / work in the building / when the bomb explode?

   A: How many people were working in the building when the bomb exploded?

   B: Approximately 55,000.

5. Six World Trade Center workers were killed. What / they do / when the bomb go off?

   A: What were they doing when the bomb went off?

   B: They were having lunch in their offices.

6. What happen to the offices / when the blast occur?

   A: What happened to the office when the blast occured?

   B: The walls crumbled and the ceilings collapsed.

7. There was a man in the garage. What / he do / when the bomb explode?

   A: What was he doing when the bomb explode?

   B: He was walking to his car.

8. What happen / when the rescue workers / bring him to the ambulance?

   A: What happened when the rescue workers brought him to the ambulance?

   B: He had a heart attack before they got him in the ambulance.

FUTURE

1 AFFIRMATIVE STATEMENTS WITH *BE GOING TO*

Read the following situations. Write a prediction. Use **be going to** *and the correct information from the box.*

crash	get a ticket	make a left turn	take a trip
eat lunch	get gas	rain	wash the car

1. Mr. Medina is carrying two suitcases toward his car.

   He's going to take a trip.

2. Ms. Marshall has a bucket of water, soap, and a sponge.

   She's going to wash the car

3. Mr. and Mrs. Johnson are driving into an Exxon service station.

   They're going to get gas.

4. Fred is driving behind a woman in a black sports car. Her left indicator

   light is flashing.

   She's going to make a left turn

5. Tiffany is driving 70 miles per hour in a 50-mile-per-hour zone. A

   police officer is right behind her.

   Armando's going to get a ticket

6. A blue Ford is driving directly toward a white Toyota. They don't have

   time to stop.

   They're going to crash

7. It's noon. The Smiths are driving into a Burger King parking lot.

   They're goin to eat lunch

8. The sky is full of dark clouds.

   It's going to rain

2 QUESTIONS WITH *BE GOING TO*

Write questions using the cues.

1. What / you / do this summer?

   A: <u>What are you going to do this summer?</u>

   B: My wife and I are going to take a trip to San Francisco.

2. How long / you / stay?

   A: <u>How long are you going to stay?</u>

   B: Just for a week.

3. you / stay at a hotel?

   A: <u>Are you going to stay at a hotel?</u>

   B: Yes. We're staying at a hotel in North Beach.

4. What / you / do in San Francisco?

   A: <u>What are you going to do in San Francisco?</u>

   B: Oh, the usual, I suppose. Sightseeing and shopping.

5. you / visit Fisherman's Wharf?

   A: <u>Are you going to visit Fisherman's Wharf?</u>

   B: Yes. We're going to take one of those city bus tours.

6. your daughter / go with you?

   A: <u>Is your daughter going to go with you?</u>

   B: No, she's going to attend summer school. Our son isn't going either.

7. What / he / do?

   A: <u>What is he going to do?</u>

   B: He got a job at Burger King.

8. When / you / leave?

   A: <u>When are you going to leave?</u>

   B: June 11.

   A: Have a good trip.

   B: Thanks.

3 AFFIRMATIVE AND NEGATIVE STATEMENTS WITH *BE GOING TO*

Look at Mr. and Mrs. Medina's boarding passes. Then read the following sentences. All of them have incorrect information. Correct the information.

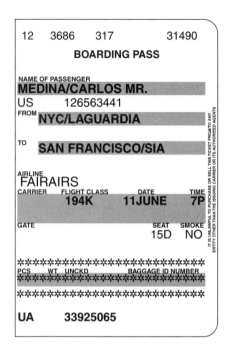

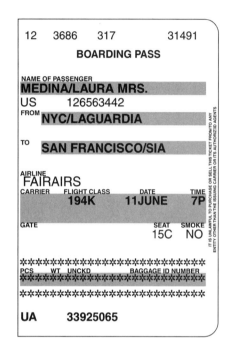

1. Mr. Medina is going to go to Los Angeles.

He isn't going to go to Los Angeles.

He's going to go to San Francisco.

2. He's going to take the train.

He isn't going to take the train.

He's going to go take an airplane

3. He's going to travel alone.

He isn't going to travel alone?

He's going with his wife

4. The Medinas are going to leave from Chicago.

They aren't going to leave from Chicago.

They're going to leave from N.Y.

(continued on next page)

5. They're going to fly US Airways.

They aren't going to fly US Airways

They're going to fly FAIRAIRS

6. They're going to leave on July 11.

They aren't going to leave on July 11

They're going to leave on June 11

7. The plane is going to depart at 7:00 A.M.

The plane isn't going to depart at 7:00 AM.

The plane is going to depart at 7:00 PM

8. The Medinas are going to sit apart.

They aren't going to sit apart

They are going to sit together

9. They are going to be in a smoking section.

They aren't going to be in a smoking section

They are going to be in a no smoking section

10. Mrs. Medina is going to sit in seat 15B.

She isn't going to sit in seat 15B

She is going to sit in 15C

---

4 **AFFIRMATIVE AND NEGATIVE STATEMENTS, QUESTIONS, AND SHORT ANSWERS WITH *WILL***

*Mrs. Medina is reading the airplane magazine. Complete this magazine interview about personal robots. Use **will** or **won't** and the verbs in parentheses ( ).*

INTERVIEWER: We all know that robots are already working in factories. But tell

us something about the future. _____Will_____ people

_____have_____ robots at home?

      1. (have)

SCIENTIST: Yes, they _____will_____. I believe that personal robots

      2.

Will *become* as common in the home as personal computers
3. (become)
are today.

INTERVIEWER: *Will* they *replace* the computer?
4. (replace)

SCIENTIST: No, they *won't replace* the computer, but one day robots
5. (replace)
will probably *operate* computers.
6. (operate)

INTERVIEWER: Amazing! What other things *will* personal robots
do?
7. (do)

SCIENTIST: Well, for one thing, they *will be* complete home
8. (be)
entertainment centers. They*'ll sing*, they*'ll*
9. (sing)
dance . . .
10. (dance)

INTERVIEWER: *Will* they *tell* jokes?
11. (tell)

SCIENTIST: Yes, they *will*! But, as with humans, they
12.
won't always *be* funny!
13. (be)

INTERVIEWER: What else *will* the personal robot *do*?
14. (do)
Will it *have* more serious uses?
15. (have)

SCIENTIST: Yes, it *will*. Robots *will* probably
16.
help care for this country's aging population. They
17. (help)
won't replace people, but they *will perform* some of the more
18. (replace) **19. (perform)**
routine activities such as vacuuming and loading the dishwasher.

INTERVIEWER: It all sounds great. Do you predict any problems?

SCIENTIST: Unfortunately, yes. Some people *won't be* happy with the
20. (be)
spread of robots. Not everyone's life *will improve*. Some people
21. (improve)
will lose their jobs to robots. And other people
22. (lose)
will create criminal robots!
23. (create)

INTERVIEWER: *Will* we *need* new laws to deal with robotic
24. (need)
crime?

SCIENTIST: I'm afraid so.

(continued on next page)

INTERVIEWER: Tell me, how _____will_____ these personal robots

_____look_____?
25. (look)

SCIENTIST: Well, they _____won't look_____ exactly like humans, but they
26. (look)

_____resemble_____ them.
27. (resemble)

INTERVIEWER: And when _____will_____ all this _____happen_____?
28. (happen)

SCIENTIST: Soon! I predict it _____will happen_____ in the very near future.
29. (happen)

---

5 RECOGNIZING THE SIMPLE PRESENT AND PRESENT PROGRESSIVE WHEN THEY REFER TO THE FUTURE

Read this article about a new play. Underline the simple present tense verbs and present progressive verbs only when they refer to the future.

A NEW PLAY

BATS

Next Wednesday <u>is</u> the first performance of *Bats*. Melissa Robins <u>is playing</u> the leading role. Robins, who lives in Italy and who is vacationing in Greece, is not available for an interview at this time. She <u>is</u>, however, <u>appearing</u> on Channel 8's "Theater Talk" sometime next month.

Although shows traditionally begin at 8:00 P.M., *Bats*, because of its length, <u>starts</u> a half-hour earlier.

Immediately <u>following</u> the opening-night performance, the company <u>is having</u> a reception in the theater lounge. Tickets are still available. Call 555-6310 for more information.

---

6 CONTRAST OF FUTURE FORMS

Read the conversations and circle the most appropriate future forms.

1. **A:** Do you know our arrival time?

   B: According to the schedule, (we arrive)/ we'll arrive at 10:45.

2. **A:** Why did you bring your computer with you?

   B: I'll do / (I'm going to do) some work while we're away.

3. A: I'm thirsty. I think I'll ask / I'm asking for a Coke.

   B: Good idea. There's the flight attendant.

4. A: Excuse me. Do you know what the weather's like in San Francisco?

   B: It's clear now, but it's raining / it's going to rain tomorrow.

5. A: Which movie will they show / are they showing?

   B: The latest *Star Wars*. Have you seen it?

6. A: Just look at those dark clouds!

   B: I see. It looks like we're going to have / we'll have some rough weather ahead.

BAD

↳ Hard

7. A: I'm tired. I think I'll take / I'm taking a little nap. Wake me when the movie begins.

   B: OK. Sweet dreams.

8. A: It's 11:00 P.M. already!

   B: I know. We're going to arrive / We arrive late.

9. A: You know, I don't think the airport buses run after midnight.

   B: I'm afraid you're right. How are we going to get / are we getting to the hotel?

10. A: Hmm. No buses. Well, that's no problem. We'll take / We're going to take a taxi instead.

   B: Good idea.

11. A: I missed the announcement. What did the captain say?

   B: He said, "Fasten your seat belts. We're landing / We'll land in about ten minutes."

12. C: How long are you going to stay / will you stay in San Francisco?

   A & B: Just a week.

   C: Well, enjoy yourselves. And thank you for flying FairAirs.

7 EDITING

Read this boy's postcard. Find and correct five mistakes in the use of future forms. The first mistake is already corrected. Note: There may be more than one way to correct the mistakes!

> ## Greetings from
> # San Francisco!
>
> Hi!
>
> I ^{'m} going to stay here for a week with my parents.
>
> We have a lot of fun things planned. Tomorrow night we'll see
>
> a play called <u>Bats</u>. Mom already bought tickets for it. The play
>
> begins at 8:00, and before that we have dinner on Fisherman's
>
> Wharf. Right now we're sitting in Golden Gate Park, but we
>
> have to leave. It has suddenly gotten very cloudy. It will rain!
>
> I call you soon.
>
> Jason

FUTURE TIME CLAUSES

❶ SIMPLE PRESENT TENSE OR FUTURE WITH *WILL*

Complete the clauses with the correct form of the verbs in parentheses ( ).
Then match each time clause to a main clause.

Time Clause	**Main Clause**
_h_ **1.** When the alarm clock _____rings_____, (ring)	**a.** they __'ll be__ very tired. (be)
_c_ **2.** As soon as the coffee ____It's____ ready, (be)	**b.** she __'ll drive__. (drive)
_g_ **3.** When they ___finish___ breakfast, (finish)	**c.** they __'ll drink__ it. (drink)
_e_ **4.** After her husband ___washes___ the dishes, (wash)	**d.** they __'ll fasten__ their seat belts. (fasten)
_d_ **5.** As soon as they ___get in___ the car, (get in)	**e.** she __'ll dry__ them. (dry)
_b_ **6.** Until he ___gets___ his driver's license, (get)	**f.** they __'ll need__ their umbrellas. (need)
_f_ **7.** Until the rain ___stops___, (stop)	**g.** they __'ll do__ the dishes. (do)
_a_ **8.** By the time the day ___is___ over, (be)	**h.** she ___'ll get up.___ (get up)

2 **SIMPLE PRESENT OR FUTURE (WILL / BE GOING TO)
AND TIME EXPRESSIONS**

*Vera is a student. Look at her future plans. Complete the sentences
below with the correct form of the verbs in parentheses ( ) and choose
the correct time expression.*

Future Plans

○   Take the TOEFL®* exam

Apply to college for next year

Finish school

Visit Aunt Isabel at Shadybrook

Get a summer job and take a computer-programming course

Fly to Brazil — Aug. 28

Get married! — Sept. 30

○   Return to the United States

TOEFL® = Test of English as a Foreign Language

---

1. Vera _____will take_____ the TOEFL exam _____before_____ she _____applies_____ to college.
   (take)   (when / before)   (apply)

2. Vera _will apply_ to college _before_ she _finishes_ school.
   (apply)   (before / after)   (finish)

3. _After_ she _finishes_ school, she'_ll visit_ her aunt.
   (Before / After)   (finish)   (visit)

4. _While_ she _works_ at a summer job, she _will take_ a course
   (Before / While)   (work)   (take)
   in computer programming.

5. She'_ll visit_ her aunt _before_ she _gets_ a summer job.
   (visit)   (while / before)   (get)

6. _When_ she _finishes_ the course, she _will fly_ to Brazil.
   (Before / When)   (finish)   (fly)

7. She'_ll get married_ _when_ she _is_ in Brazil.
   (get married)   (when / before)   (be)

8. She'_ll return_ to the United States _After_ she _gets married_.
   (return)   (before / after)   (get married)

❸ SIMPLE PRESENT TENSE OR FUTURE

Vera's aunt lives at Shadybrook Retirement Village. Complete this ad for Shadybrook. Use the correct form of the verbs in parentheses ( ).

> *Shadybrook*
> *Retirement Village*
>
> What _____will_____ you _____do_____ when you
> _____retire_____ ? Where _____will_____ you _____go_____ when
> **1. (do)**
> **2. (retire)**   **3. (go)**
> you finally _____have_____ all that free time?
> **4. (have)**
> By the time you _____turn_____ 65, you probably '_will want_'
> **5. (turn)**   **6. (want)**
> to make some major life changes. Here at *Shadybrook Retirement*
>
> *Village,* you can enjoy swimming, tennis, golf, and much more.
>
> Come and see for yourself. After you _____visit_____ us, you
> **7. (visit)**
> _won't want_ to leave!
> **8. (not want)**

❹ SENTENCE COMBINING

Combine these sentences. Use the simple present tense and future forms
*(**will / be going to**).*

1. Vera will finish her summer job. Then she's going to fly to Brazil.

   _____Vera is going to fly to Brazil_____ after _____she finishes her summer job._____

2. Vera will save enough money from her summer job. Then she's going to buy a plane
   ticket.
   (Enseguida)
   As soon as _____She save enough money, she'll buy a plane_____
   _____ticket_____
   when
   Until (hasta)

(continued on next page)

3. Vera's going to buy presents for her family. Then she's going to go home.

   Before _she goes home, she's going to buy presents for her family._

4. Vera will arrive at the airport. Her father will be there to drive her home.

   When _she arrives at the airport, her father will be there to drive her home_

5. Vera and her father will get home. They'll immediately have dinner.

   As soon as _They get home, they'll immediately have dinner_

6. They'll finish dinner. Then Vera will give her family the presents.

   Vera will give her family the presents after _They finish dinner_

7. Vera's brother will wash the dishes, and Vera's sister will dry them.

   Vee's brother will wash the dishes while _Vera's sister dries them_

8. The whole family will stay up talking. Then the clock will strike midnight.

   The whole family will stay up talking until _the clock strikes midnight_

9. They'll all feel very tired. Then they'll go to bed.

   By the time _they go to bed, they'll feel very tired._

10. Vera's head will hit the pillow, and she'll fall asleep immediately.

   she'll fall asleep immediately as soon as _her head hits the pillow_

5 PERSONALIZATION

Complete these sentences with information about your own future plans.

1. As soon as _____, I'll go to bed.

2. Before I take a break, _____.

3. Until _____, I'll stay in school.

4. When I save enough money, _____.

5. I won't _____ before I _____.

6. _____ after _____.

7. _____ while _____.

8. When I finish this exercise, _____.

WH- QUESTIONS:
SUBJECT AND PREDICATE

1 SUBJECT QUESTIONS

Ask questions about the words in italics. Use **What**, **Whose**, **Who**, *or*
How many.

1. *Something* happened last night.

    What happened last night?

2. *Someone's* phone rang at midnight.

_____

3. *Someone* was calling for Michelle.

_____

4. *Someone* was having a party.

_____

5. *Some number of* people left the party.

_____

6. *Something* surprised them.

_____

7. *Someone's* friend called the police.

_____

8. *Some number of* police arrived.

_____

9. *Something* happened next.

_____

10. *Someone* told the police about a theft.

_____

(continued on next page)

11. *Someone's* jewelry disappeared.

_____

12. *Some number of* necklaces vanished.

_____

2 PREDICATE QUESTIONS

Use the cues to write questions about Megan Knight, an accountant in
Texas. Then match each question to its correct answer.

Questions	Answers
1. Where / she / live?	**a.** Two years.
<u>Where does she live?</u> _e_	
2. How many rooms / her apartment / have?	**b.** By bus.
_____ ____	
3. How much rent / she / pay?	**c.** The first of the month.
_____ ____	
4. When / she / pay the rent?	**d.** Ling, Jackson, & Drew, Inc.
_____ ____	
5. Who / she / live with?	**e.** In Texas.
_____ ____	
6. What / she / do?	**f.** Five and a half.
_____ ____	
7. Which company / she / work for?	**g.** She's an accountant.
_____ ____	
8. How long / she / plan to stay there?	**h.** Her sister.
_____ ____	
9. How / she / get to work?	**i.** Because she doesn't like to drive.
_____ ____	
10. Why / she / take the bus?	**j.** About $800 a month.
_____ ____	

❸ SUBJECT AND PREDICATE QUESTIONS

Megan wrote a letter to her friend, Janice. The letter got wet, and now Janice can't read some parts of it. What questions does Janice ask to get the missing information?

Dear Janice,
   Hi! I just moved to ____ ¹ I left Chicago because ____.² ____ ³ moved with me, and we are sharing an apartment. I got a job in a ____.⁴ It started ____.⁵ The people seem nice.
   Our apartment is great. It has ____ ⁶ rooms. ____ of the rooms came with carpeting, but two of them have beautiful wood floors. The rent isn't too high, either. We each pay $ ____ a month.

   We need to buy som ____.⁹ ____'s¹⁰ brother wants to visit her, so we really need an extra bed.
   By the way, ____ ¹¹ called last Sunday. I also spoke to ____.¹² They want to visit us in ____.¹³
   Would you like to come, too? Is that a good time for you? There's plenty of room because ____.¹⁴ Write and let me know.
                              Love,
                              Megan

1. Where did you move?
2. _____
3. _____
4. _____
5. _____
6. _____
7. _____
8. _____
9. _____
10. _____
11. _____
12. _____
13. _____
14. _____

U N I T

9 REFLEXIVE AND RECIPROCAL PRONOUNS

1 REFLEXIVE PRONOUNS

Write the reflexive pronouns.

1. I   _____myself_____

2. my grandfather   _____

3. the children   _____

4. the class   _____

5. my aunt   _____

6. you   _____ OR _____

7. people   _____

8. life   _____

9. my parents   _____

10. we   _____

2 REFLEXIVE AND RECIPROCAL PRONOUNS

Circle the correct pronouns to complete these sentences.

1. Cindi and Jim phone (each other)/ themselves every weekend.

2. They have worked with each other / themselves for five years.

3. Cindi herself / himself has been with the same company for ten years.

4. It's a nice place to work. All of the employees consider one another / themselves lucky to be working there.

5. They respect each other / each other's opinions.

6. The boss herself / itself is very nice.

7. She tells her employees, "Don't push <u>themselves / yourselves</u> too hard!"

8. Cindi enjoys the job <u>herself / itself</u>, but she especially likes her co-workers.

9. My brother and I are considering applying for a job there <u>myself / ourselves</u>.

10. We talk to <u>each other / ourselves</u> about it when we jog together.

❸ REFLEXIVE AND RECIPROCAL PRONOUNS

Read the conversations. Complete the summary with appropriate reflexive and reciprocal pronouns and forms of the verbs in parentheses.

1.   **JOYCE:** This party is a lot of fun.
     HANK: I've never danced with so many people in my life!

   SUMMARY: Joyce and Hank <u>   *are enjoying themselves*   </u>.
                                                                    (enjoy)

2.   **CARA:** You know, you're really easy to talk to.
     MAX: I feel the same way. I feel like we've known each other a long time.

   SUMMARY: Cara and Max _____ company.
                                                        (enjoy)

3.   **GINA:** I'm so glad you could come. There are food and drinks on that table over there. Why don't you take a plate and get some?
     CHEN: Thanks. I will. It all looks delicious.

   SUMMARY: Chen _____.
                                                                 (help)

4.   **AMY:** OK, Amy. Now don't be shy. Go over and talk to him.
     TIM: Come on, Tim. You can do it. She's looking in your direction. Just go on over.

   SUMMARY: Amy and Tim _____.
                                                               (talk)

5.   **AMY:** Hi. I'm Amy.
     TIM: Hi. I'm Tim.

   SUMMARY: Amy and Tim _____.
                                                           (introduce)

6.   **AMY:** So, how do you know Gina?
     TIM: Oh, Gina and I were in the same class. What about you?

   SUMMARY: Amy and Tim _____.
                                                               (talk)

7.   **PAT:** Did you come with Doug?
     LAURA: No. Doug couldn't make it, but he let me use his car.

   SUMMARY: Laura _____.
                                                               (drive)

8.   **LIZ:** I'm sorry to hear about your job, Hank.
     HANK: I think I didn't take it seriously enough, but I've learned my lesson. I'll do better next time.

   SUMMARY: Hank _____.
                                                           (blame)

(continued on next page)

9. **RON:** We were late because you forgot the address.
    MIA: It's not my fault. You never gave me the slip of paper!

SUMMARY: Ron and Mia _____.
                                          (criticize)

10. **LIZ:** It was a wonderful party. Thanks for inviting me.
    GINA: Thanks for coming. And thank you for the lovely flowers.

SUMMARY: Liz and Gina _____.
                                            (thank)

---

④ EDITING

Read Liz's journal entry. Find and correct nine mistakes in the use of reflexive and reciprocal pronouns. The first mistake is already corrected.

April 25

              myself
                                          each other

I really enjoyed ~~me~~ at Gina's party! Hank was there and we talked to ~~ourselves~~

quite a bit. He's a little depressed about losing his job. He thinks it's all his own

                                           me

fault, and he blames him for the whole thing. Hank introduced ~~myself~~ to several of

his friends. I spoke a lot to this one woman, Cara. We have a lot of things in

common, and after just an hour, we felt like we had known each other~~'s~~ forever.

  herself

Cara, ~~himself~~, is a computer programmer, just like me.

    At first I was nervous about going to the party alone. I sometimes feel a little

                                          myself

uncomfortable when I'm in a social situation by ~~oneself~~. But this time was

different. Before I went, I kept telling myself to relax. My roommate, too, kept

     me   *yourself*

telling ~~myself~~, "Don't be so hard on ~~you~~! Just have fun!" That's what I advised

                                           each other/one other

Hank to do, too. Before we left the party, Hank and I promised ~~us~~ to keep in touch.

I hope to see him again soon.

PHRASAL VERBS

① PARTICLES

Complete the chart.

Phrasal Verb	Definition
1. take ___off___	*remove*
2. figure ___out___	*solve*
3. go ___on___	*continue*
4. call ___off___	*cancel*
5. call ___on___	*phone*
6. fill ___out___	*complete*
7. turn ___down___	*reject*
8. point ___out___	*indicate*
9. grow ___up___	*become an adult*
10. give ___up___	*quit*
11. help ___out___	*assist*
12. blow ___up___	*explode*
13. look ___out___	*be careful*
14. come ___in___	*enter*
15. work ___out___	*exercise*

heads up - cae en la cabeza

2 PHRASAL VERBS

Complete the handout. Use the correct phrasal verbs from the box.

do over	hand in	help out	look over	look up
pick out	pick up	set up	talk over	write up

Science 101   Instructions for Writing the Term Paper   Prof. Cho

pick out, too

1. ___Pick up___ a list of topics from the science department secretary.

2. ___pick out___ a topic that interests you. (If you are having problems choosing a topic, I'll be glad to ___help___ you ___out___.)

3. Go to the library. ___look up___ information on your chosen topic.

stablish
4. ___Set up___ an appointment with me to ___talk over___ your topic.

5. ___Write up___ your first draft.

6. ___look___ it ___over___ carefully. Check for accuracy of facts, spelling, and grammar errors.

7. ___do___ your report ___over___ if necessary.

8. ___hand___ it ___in___ by May 28.

3 PHRASAL VERBS AND OBJECT PRONOUNS

Complete these conversations between roommates. Use phrasal verbs and pronouns.

1. **A:** I haven't picked up the list of topics for our science paper yet.

   B: I'll ___pick it up___ for you. I'm going to the science office this afternoon.

2. **A:** Hey, guys. We've really got to clean up the kitchen. It's a mess.

   B: It's my turn to _____. I'll do it after dinner.

3. **A:** Did you remember to call your mom up?

   B: Oops! I'll _____ tonight.

4. A: Hey. Can you turn down that music? I'm trying to concentrate.

    B: Sorry. I'll _____ right away.

5. A: It's after 9:00. Do you think we should wake John up?

    B: Don't _____. He said he wanted to sleep late.

6. A: Professor Cho turned down my science topic.

    B: Really? Why did she _____?

7. A: When do we have to hand in our reports?

    B: We have to _____ by Friday.

8. A: I wanted to drop off my report this afternoon, but I'm not going to have time.

    B: I can _____ for you. I have an appointment with

    Professor Cho at noon.

❹ WORD ORDER

Professor Cho made a list of things to do with her class. Unscramble the words to make sentences. In some cases, more than one answer is possible.

1. sit / with the class / down _____ Sit down with the class. _____

2. the homework problems / up / bring _____

3. out / common mistakes / point _____

4. them / over / talk _____

5. go / to the next unit / on _____

6. Friday's class / off / call _____

7. up / the final exam questions / make _____

8. them / out / hand _____

5 EDITING

Read this student's letter. Find and correct eleven mistakes in the use of phrasal verbs. The first mistake is already corrected.

Dear Katy,

How are things going? I'm already into the second month of the spring semester, and I've got a lot of work to do. For science class, I have to write a term paper. The
professor made ~~over~~ up a list of possible topics. After looking over them, I think I've picked one out. I'm going to write about chimpanzees. I've already gone to the library to look some information about them in the encyclopedia up. I found up some very interesting facts.

Did you know that their hands look very much like their feet, and that they have fingernails and toenails? Their thumbs and big toes are "opposable." This makes it easy for them to pick things out with both their fingers and toes. Their arms are longer than their legs. This helps out them, too, because they can reach out to fruit growing on thin branches that could not otherwise support their weight. Adult males weigh between 90 and 115 pounds, and they are about four feet high when they stand out.

Like humans, chimpanzees are very social. They travel in groups called "communities." Mothers bring out their chimps, who stay with them until about the age of seven. Even after the chimps have grown up, there is still a lot of contact with other chimpanzees.

I could go on, but I need to stop writing now so I can clean out my room (it's a mess!) a little before going to bed. It's late already, and I have to get early up tomorrow morning for my 9:00 a.m. class.

Please write and let me know how you are. Or call up me sometime! It would be great to speak to you.

Best,

Tony

ABILITY:
CAN, COULD, BE ABLE TO

 **AFFIRMATIVE AND NEGATIVE STATEMENTS
WITH *CAN* AND *COULD***

Read about this student's ability in English. Then complete the statements for each item.

Student's Name _Fernando Ochoa_

English Language Ability Questionnaire

Skill	Now	Before This Course
1. understand conversational English	✓	✗
2. understand recorded announcements	✗	✗
3. read an English newspaper	✓	✓
4. read an English novel	✗	✗
5. speak on the phone	✓	✗
6. speak with a group of people	✓	✗
7. write a social letter	✓	✗
8. write a business letter	✗	✗
9. order a meal in English	✓	✓
10. go shopping	✓	✓

1. Before this course he _couldn't understand conversational English._

   Now _he can understand conversational English._

2. He _couldn't understand recorded announcements_ before the course,

   and he still _can't understand them._

49

(continued on next page)

3. He _____ now, and he _____

   before, too.

4. He _____ before the course, and he still _____.

5. Now he _____, but before the course he_____.

6. Before the course, he _____, but now he _____.

7. Before the course, he _____. Now he_____.

8. _____

9. _____

10. _____

SUMMARY: Fernando _____ do a lot more now than he

_____ before the course.

❷ QUESTIONS AND ANSWERS WITH *CAN* AND *COULD*

Complete this interview with another student.

1. (speak / any other languages?)

   A: <u>Can you speak any other languages?</u> _____

   B: _____<u>Yes, I can.</u>_____ I speak two other languages.

2. (What / languages / speak?)

   A: <u>what languages can you speak?</u>

   B: Spanish and French.

3. (speak Spanish / when you were a child?)

   A: ~~could you were~~ <u>Could you speak Spanish, when you were a child?</u>

   B: <u>No I couldn't</u> I learned it as an adult.

4. (speak French?)

   A: <u>Could you speak french?</u>

   B: <u>Yes, I could.</u> We spoke French some of the time at home.

5. (Before you came here / understand spoken English?)

Before you came here,

A: Could you understand spoken English ~~before came~~

B: No, I couldn't _____ I didn't understand anything!

6. What about now? (understand song lyrics?)

A: Can you understand song lyrics?

B: Yes, I can _____ Especially if I listen to them more than once.

7. (Before this course / write a business letter in English?)

A: Before this course, could you writes a business letter *in English?*

B: No, I couldn't _____ But I used to write in English to my friends.

8. Enough about languages. Tell me some more about yourself. For example,

(drive a car before you came here?)

A: Could you drive a car before you came here?

B: No, I couldn't _____ I was too young.

9. (drive a car now?)

A: Can you drive a car now?

B: No, I can't _____ I still haven't learned.

10. (swim?) We're not too far from the beach here.

A: Can you swim

B: Yes, I can _____ I've been swimming since I was a little kid.

11. What about surfing? (surf before you came here?)

A: Could

B: No, I couldn't _____ But I learned to surf the first month I was here.

12. (What / do now / that / not do before?)

A: What can you do now that you couldn't do before

B: Oh! I ___ can~~t~~ do _____ a lot of things now that I

couldn't ~~to~~ do _____ before.

3 AFFIRMATIVE AND NEGATIVE STATEMENTS WITH *BE ABLE TO*

Complete this article about hearing loss. Use the correct form of **be able to**
and the verbs in parentheses ( ).

There are more than 26 million people in the United States who have some degree of hearing loss. There are two major types of hearing loss.

1. **Sound Sensitivity Loss.** People with this kind of loss _____ are not able to hear _____
   1. (not hear)

   soft sounds—a whisper or a bird singing, for example. However, when sounds are

   loud enough, they _are able to interpret_ them correctly.
   2. (interpret)

2. **Sound Discrimination Loss.** People with this kind of hearing loss

   are not able to distinguish one sound from another. As a result of this, they
   3. (not distinguish)

   are not able to understand speech—even when it is loud enough for them to
   4. (not understand)

   hear.

   How do people with hearing disabilities cope in a hearing world? Most people with

   hearing impairments _are able to hear_ some sounds. Since the
   5. (hear)

   widespread availability of the hearing aid, many people

   are able to regain some of their ability to hear. Some people with
   6. (regain)

   hearing disabilities _are able to read_ lips. But, at best, lip reading is
   7. (read)

   only 30 to 50 percent effective. Even a good lip reader _is not able to recognize_
   8. (not recognize)

   all the sounds. Just ask someone to silently mouth the words *pat*, *bat*, and *mat*. They

   sound different, but they all *look* the same. Besides, the human eye

   is not able to work fast enough to process speech by vision alone. By
   9. (not work)

   far the most successful form of communication is signing—the use of sign language.

   People with hearing impairments _are able to communicate_ successfully with
   10. (communicate)

   others who know this language.

④ QUESTIONS AND SHORT ANSWERS WITH *BE ABLE TO*

Sensitivity to sound is measured in decibels. Look at this chart. It shows the decibel measurements of some common sounds.

0 decibels	softest sound a typical ear can hear
20 decibels	a whisper
45 decibels	soft conversational speech
55 decibels	loud conversational speech
65 decibels	loud music from the radio
75 decibels	city traffic
100 decibels	loud factory noise
110 decibels	loud amplified rock band
120 decibels	loud power tool
140 decibels	jet engine at takeoff

Source: Rezen and Hausman, *Coping with Hearing Loss: A Guide for Adults and Their Families,* New York: Dembner Books, 1985.

Mary has a hearing loss of 50 decibels. This means she will not be able to hear sounds that have a loudness of 50 decibels or less. Ask and answer these questions about what Mary will be able to hear at the party she is going to.

1. **A:** _____Will she be able to hear_____ a whisper?

   B: _____No, she won't._____

2. **A:** _____ loud music?

   B: _____

3. **A:** _____ a soft conversation?

   B: _____

4. **A:** _____ loud traffic?

   B: _____

5. **A:** _____ a loud conversation?

   B: _____

5 CONTRAST: *CAN* AND *BE ABLE TO*

Read this information about a well-known actress who is deaf.
Complete it with the correct form of **can** *or* **be able to** *and the verbs in*
parentheses ( ). Use **can** *or* **could** *when possible.*

Actress Marlee Matlin _____could hear_____ at
1. (hear)
birth but lost her hearing at the age of 18 months as a result

of a childhood illness. By the age of five, she

_____could read_____ lips. Shortly after that, she
2. (read)
mastered sign language. At first, Matlin felt angry and

frightened by her hearing impairment. "I wanted to be perfect,

and I __could not accept__ my deafness," she said during an interview. With
3. (not accept)
time, however, she __was able to learn__ to accept it.
4. (learn)

Matlin began her acting career at the age of eight, when she performed in theater for the

deaf. In 1986, she received an Oscar nomination for best actress in the Hollywood film,

Children of a Lesser God. In the movie she played the role of an angry woman who was

deaf and did not want to speak. For Matlin, however, speaking is very important. At the

Oscar ceremonies, she __was able to accept__ her award verbally. It was the first time
5. (accept)
the public heard her speak. "It's what I wanted to do, because a lot of people all over the

world __could see__ me for who I am," she said. Matlin was worried however.
6. (see)
"What other roles __~~could~~ will__ I __be able to do__ in the future?"
7. (do)
she asked.

Since her Oscar award, Matlin has appeared in another Hollywood movie, a television

movie, and has co-starred in her own TV series. One reviewer said about Matlin, "She

__can do__ more saying nothing than most people
8. (do)
__can do__ talking." Matlin doesn't think of herself as a "deaf actress."
9. (do)
She is an "actress who happens to be deaf." She __has been able to master__ both the deaf
10. (master)
and hearing worlds. Since recent intensive speech training, she __has been able to speak__
11. (speak)
very clearly, and in the future, she hopes she __will be able to get__ roles that are not
12. (get)
specifically written for people with hearing impairments.

6 EDITING

Read this student's composition. Find and correct seven mistakes in the
use of **can** *and* **be able to**. *The first mistake is already corrected.*

                                                couldn't

Before I came to this country I ~~can't~~ do many things in English. For example, I

couldn't follow a conversation if many people were talking at the same time. I

remember one occasion at a party. I wasn't able understand a word! I felt so

uncomfortable. Finally, my aunt came to pick me up, and I could leave the party.

    Today I can to understand much better. Since last month I can practice a lot. I

am taking classes at the adult center. My teacher is very good. She can explains

things well, and she always gives us the chance to talk a lot in class. I can do a lot

now, and I think in a few more months I can do even more.

7 PERSONALIZATION

Look at the English Language Ability Questionnaire in Exercise 1. Write
sentences about your English ability now and before this course.

1. _____

    _____

2. _____

    _____

3. _____

    _____

4. _____

    _____

UNIT 12

PERMISSION:
MAY, COULD, CAN,
DO YOU MIND IF . . . ?

❶ QUESTIONS AND RESPONSES

Match these classroom questions and responses.

Questions	Responses
1. __d__ Do you mind if I bring my friends to class?	**a.** Certainly. The key to the rest room is hanging on the wall.
2. _____ May I ask a question?	**b.** Not at all.
3. _____ Do you mind if I tape the lesson?	**c.** Sure. I hope I can answer it.
4. _____ Could I open the window?	**d.** Actually, I do mind. It's already pretty crowded.
5. _____ Can we review Unit 4?	**e.** Sure. But remember, you don't have to look up every word.
6. _____ May I leave the room?	**f.** I'm afraid we can't. We're running out of time.
7. _____ Could we use our dictionaries?	**g.** Sure. But please remember to return it.
8. _____ Could I borrow a pen?	**h.** Go right ahead. It's quite warm in here.

❷ QUESTIONS

Read the situations. Complete the questions.

1. You want to open the window.

   May ___I open the window?_____

2. Your whole class wants to review Unit 6.

   Could _____

3. You want to borrow a classmate's pen.

Can _____

4. You want to look at someone's class notes.

Do you mind if _____

5. You want to come late to the next class.

Do you mind if _____

6. Your husband wants to come to the next class with you.

Could _____

7. You want to ask a question.

May _____

8. You and a classmate would like to use a dictionary.

Can _____

9. You and your classmates want to leave five minutes early.

Could _____

10. Your sister wants to go on the class trip with the rest of the class.

Do you mind if _____

③ PERSONALIZATION

Imagine that you are in class. Read the following situations. Ask your teacher for permission to do something.

1. You don't understand something the teacher is saying.

_____

2. You don't feel well.

_____

3. Your cousin from (your country) is going to visit you for a week.

_____

4 AFFIRMATIVE AND NEGATIVE STATEMENTS

Look at the flier. Complete the statements. Use the words in parentheses ( ).

CLASS TRIP

You are invited to our annual class picnic on Sunday,

May 26, at Glenwood State Park.

Food and Beverages Welcome, but

No Glass Containers Please!

Bus Tickets $5.00 (check or cash)

Advance Purchase Only • No Refunds

Bring a Friend!

---

1. You _____may bring_____ a friend.
(may / bring)

2. You _____ your own food.
(can / bring)

3. You _____ juice from a glass bottle at the picnic.
(can / drink)

4. You _____ for your bus ticket by check.
(can / pay)

5. You _____ for your bus ticket by cash.
(can / pay)

6. You _____ for your ticket by credit card.
(may / pay)

7. You _____ your bus ticket on the day of the trip.
(may / purchase)

8. You _____ a refund.
(can / get)

⑤ EDITING

*Read this professor's response to an e-mail from one of his students. (The professor's answers are in **bold** print.) Find and correct five mistakes in making and responding to requests. The first mistake is already corrected.*

Subj: missed classes—Reply
Date: 04-22-01   11:22:43 EST
From: aolinsky@bryant.edu
To: Timbotwo@hotline.com

>>>Timbotwo@hotline.com> 04/22/01   9:05am>>>

Professor Olinsky—

                                              take

I've been sick for the past two days. That's why I missed the last test. May I ~~taking~~ a

make up exam?

Yes. If you bring a doctor's note.

Could my brother comes to class and take notes for me on Tuesday?

Yes, he could.

Do you mind when he tapes the class for me?

Not at all. He's welcome to tape the class.

One last request—I know I missed some handouts. May I have please copies of them?

Sure. I'll give them to your brother on Tuesday.

Thanks a lot.

Tim

13 REQUESTS: WILL, WOULD, COULD, CAN, WOULD YOU MIND . . . ?

1 REQUESTS AND RESPONSES

Match these office requests and responses.

Requests

1. __d__ Could you meet me tomorrow at 8:00 A.M.?

2. _____ Will you please type this memo for me?

3. _____ Could you show me how to copy an electronic file?

4. _____ Would you please spell your last name for me?

5. _____ Would you mind mailing this letter for me?

6. _____ Can you cancel tomorrow's meeting for me? I have to go out of town.

7. _____ Will you shut the window, please?

8. _____ Would you get that box down from the closet?

9. _____ Could you get the phone for me?

10. _____ Can you give me Doug Johnson's e-mail address?

Responses

a. I'd be glad to. When do you need it?

b. Sure. It is pretty cold in here.

c. Of course I can. When would you like to reschedule it?

d. I'm sorry. I have an early morning dentist appointment.

e. Sure. It's DJohn@iol.com.

f. Sure. . . . Hello, J and R Equities.

g. Sure. It's M-A-R-D-J-A-I-T.

h. Sorry, but I'm not familiar with that software program.

i. I'd like to, but it's too heavy for me to lift.

j. Not at all.

Write the numbers of the requests that were granted: __2,_____

Write the numbers of the requests that were refused: _____

2 REQUESTS

These conversations take place in an office. Complete them, using the phrases in the box.

~~answer the phone~~	lend me $5.00
come to my office	mail a letter
explain this note to me	open the window
get Frank's phone number	pick up a sandwich
keep the noise down	stay late tonight

1. **A:** Could you_____<u>answer the phone</u>_____? My hands are full.

   B: Sure. I'll get it.

2. **A:** Would you mind _____? It's really hot in here.

   B: No, not at all.

3. **A:** Can you please _____ for me?

   B: Certainly. I pass the post office on my way home.

4. **A:** I'm going to the coffee shop. Can I get you anything?

   B: Could you _____ for me?

5. **A:** Would you mind _____? I really have to get this report

   done by tomorrow.

   B: I'm sorry, but I have to visit my aunt in the hospital.

6. **A:** Will you _____, please? I can't hear myself think!

   B: Sorry!

7. **A:** Can you _____ when you have the chance?

   B: Sure. I'll be right there.

8. **A:** Would you _____ for me?

   B: It's 555-4345.

9. **A:** Would you mind _____?

   B: Not at all. What is it that you don't understand?

10. **A:** Could you _____?

    B: Oh, I'm sorry. I'm short on cash.

(continued on next page)

❸ EDITING

Read these office notes. Find and correct six mistakes in the use of requests. The first mistake is already corrected.

1.

Meng,

file
Would you ~~filed~~ these, please?

Thanks.

R.L.

2.

write it down

Hi Ted,

Could you please remember to turn off the lights when you leave?

Thanks,

Lynn

3.

HANK,
please
WILL YOU ~~RETURN~~
return
~~PLEASE~~ THE
STAPLER?

BRAD

4.

leave
Melida,

Can you make 5 copies of these pages, ~~please?~~
please
Thanks.

Ellen

5.

John,

Would you mind
leaving
~~leave~~ the finished
report on my desk?

Roy

6.

Celia,

Could you please remember to lock the door.?

Thank you.

Diana

7.

Would you please ~~to~~ call Ms. Rivera before the end of the day?

Thanks,
JF

8.

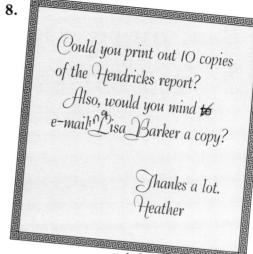

Could you print out 10 copies of the Hendricks report? Also, would you mind ~~to~~ e-mailing Lisa Barker a copy?

Thanks a lot.
Heather

would you mind sending an e-mail lisa Barker a copy?

---

4 PERSONALIZATION

Write one request that you would like to make of each of the following people.

1. (To your teacher) _____

2. (To a classmate) _____

3. (To a friend) _____

4. (To your boss) _____

5. (To your landlord) _____

6. (To _____) _____

UNIT

14 ADVICE: SHOULD, OUGHT TO, HAD BETTER

 QUESTIONS AND ANSWERS WITH *SHOULD*

Read this invitation. Use the information in the invitation to complete the phone conversation.

YOU ARE INVITED TO A PARTY!

FOR: *Scott's SURPRISE graduation barbecue*

DATE: *June 11*

TIME: *2:00 P.M. sharp!*

PLACE: *20 Greenport Avenue*

RSVP by May 15. Please don't call here!

Leave a message at 555-3234.

No Gifts, please!

(but please bring something to drink)

WANDA: Hi, Tania.

TANIA: Hi, Wanda. What's up?

WANDA: Aunt Rosa's having a graduation party for Scott. She didn't have

your new address, so she asked me to call and invite you. It's on

June 11. Can you come?

TANIA: Sure. Just give me all the information. (What time / be there?)

What time should I be there?
1.

WANDA: Let's see. I have the invitation right here.

You should be there at 2:00 P.M. sharp.
2.

TANIA: (What / wear?)

What should I wear?
3.

WANDA: Something casual. It's a barbecue.

TANIA: (bring a gift?)

Should I bring a ~~drink~~ gift?
4.

WANDA: No, you shouldn't The invitation says "no gifts."
5.

TANIA: OK. What about food? (bring something to eat or drink?)

Should I bring something to eat or drink?
6.

WANDA: Yes, you should.
7.

Oh, and the invitation says "RSVP." In other words, Aunt Rosa wants a response.

TANIA: (When / I respond?)

When should I respond?
8.

WANDA: You should by May 15
9.

TANIA: (call Aunt Rosa?)

Should I call Aunt Rosa?
10.

WANDA: No, you shouldn't I forgot to tell you. It's a surprise party!
11.

TANIA: OK. (Who / call?)

Who should I call?
12.

WANDA: You leave a message at 555-3234.
13.

TANIA: Fine. Sounds like fun. I'll see you there. Thanks for calling.

WANDA: No problem. See you there.

2 AFFIRMATIVE AND NEGATIVE STATEMENTS WITH *HAD BETTER*

*Friends are giving Scott advice about looking for a job. Complete the advice. Use **had better** or **had better not** and the appropriate verbs from the box.*

arrive	can	dress	have	~~look at~~	tell	write
ask	chew	go	leave	stare	thank	

1. _____ You'd better look at _____ the newspaper want ads every day.

2. _____ everyone you know that you are looking for a job. "Networking" is one of the best ways to find employment.

3. _____ your old job before you find a new one. That way you'll always have some money coming in.

4. _____ late for a job interview.

5. _____ a good resume.

6. _____ nicely when you go on an interview. Don't wear your jeans!

7. _____ gum during an interview.

8. _____ call the interviewer by his or her first name. Use *Mr.* or *Ms.* unless the interviewer tells you that it is OK to be less formal.

9. _____ at the floor! Remember to make eye contact with the interviewer.

10. _____ for too much money right away. You can always get a raise after you begin.

11. _____ the interviewer at the end of the interview.

12. _____ on a lot of interviews. It's good practice.

13. _____ a lot of patience. It can take a long time.

❸ QUESTIONS AND ANSWERS: *SHOULD, OUGHT TO, AND HAD BETTER*

Scott is getting ready for a job interview. Complete his conversation with a friend. Use **should**, **ought to**, *and* **had better**. *Sometimes more than one answer is possible.*

SCOTT: ___Should I wear___ my green suit?
1. (wear)

DENNIS: I don't think so. I think ___You should wear___ your navy blue one. It's
2. (wear)
more conservative.

SCOTT: ___Should I tell___ my boss about the interview?
3. (tell)

DENNIS: No. ___You'd better wait___ until you get a job before you say anything
4. (wait)
to your old boss.

SCOTT: I think we're going out for lunch after the interview.
___should I offer___ to pay?
5. (offer)

DENNIS: I don't think so. ___You shouldn't pay___ for your lunch. The interviewer
6. (pay)
usually does that.

SCOTT: ___Should I write___ a thank-you note after the interview?
7. (write)

DENNIS: That's always a good idea.

SCOTT: When ___should I send___ it?
8. (send)

DENNIS: ___You ought to wait___ a few days. That way you can always include
9. (wait)
something you forgot to say during the interview.

SCOTT: Well, ___I'd better not forget___ to say anything important!
10. (not forget)

DENNIS: Try to relax. I'm sure you'll do fine.

SCOTT: I hope so. ___Should I call___ you after the interview?
11. (call)

DENNIS: ___You'd better call___ me or I'll never speak to you again!
12. (call)

4 EDITING

Read this letter. Find and correct five mistakes in the use of modals giving advice. The first mistake is already corrected.

Dear Scott,

Congratulations on your graduation! Your aunt and I are very proud of you.

I hear you are looking for a job. You know, you really ~~oughta~~ speak *(ought to OR should)*

to your cousin Mike. He's had *(He has)* a lot of experience in this area. You

shouldn't ~~taking~~ *(take)* the first job they offer you. You've better give *(You'd)*

yourself a lot of time to find something you'll enjoy. It's important to

be happy with what you do.

Maybe you should speak to a job counselor. In any case, you

~~oughtn't~~ *(shouldn't)* rush into anything! Should I ask Mike to call you? He really

should ~~gets~~ *(get)* in touch with you about this.

Well, that's enough advice for one letter.

All my love,

Uncle Ed

5 PERSONALIZATION

A friend of yours is very unhappy at his or her job. Give your friend some advice.

1. _____
2. _____
3. _____
4. _____
5. _____

SUGGESTIONS:
LET'S, COULD, WHY DON'T . . . ?,
WHY NOT . . . ?,
HOW ABOUT . . . ?

1 SUGGESTIONS

*Match the two halves of each suggestion. Notice the
end punctuation—period (.) or question mark (?).*

1. __c__ My feet hurt. Why don't we   **a.** going to a movie?

2. _____ The weather's terrible. How   **b.** have a cup of coffee.
about

3. _____ We have an hour before the   **c.** take a taxi?
show starts. We could

4. _____ You look exhausted. Why   **d.** go to the beach.
don't I

5. _____ This concert is terrible. Let's   **e.** getting a slice of pizza?
not

6. _____ I'm really hungry. How about   **f.** change hotels?

7. _____ There's so much to see! How   **g.** meet you back at the hotel?
about

8. _____ If John's unhappy at the Blue   **h.** buy some souvenirs there.
Water Inn, why doesn't he

9. _____ It's going to be hot   **i.** taking a walking tour?
tomorrow. Let's

10. _____ There's a gift shop. Maybe   **j.** stay until the end.
we could

❷ PUNCTUATION

Circle the correct phrase in italics to complete these conversations between tourists on vacation. Add the correct punctuation—period (.) or question mark (?).

1. **A:** I'm exhausted. We've been walking for hours.

   B: How about /(Why don't we) sit on that bench for a while ___?___

2. **A:** I'm almost out of film.

   B: There's a drugstore over there. (Maybe you could)/ Let's not get film there __.__

3. **A:** It would be nice to see some of the countryside.

   B: Let's / How about rent a car __.__

4. **A:** Why not /(How about) taking a bus tour __?__

   B: That's a good idea. It's less expensive than renting a car.

5. **A:** I want to take a picture of that building.(Why don't you)/ How about stand in front
   of it __?__

   B: OK.

6. **A:** We have an hour before we have to meet the rest of our tour group.

   B: (Let's)/ Let's not get a cup of coffee in that cafe __.__

   A: Good idea. I could use something to drink.

7. **A:** I heard it's going to rain tomorrow.

   B: (Maybe we could)/ How about go to a museum __.__

8. **A:** I really need to get a better map of the city.

   B: (Why don't you)/ Let's not stop at that tourist information office __?__
   I'm sure they have maps.

9. **A:** I don't know what to get for my daughter.

   B: Why don't you /(How about) getting one of those sweatshirts __?__

10. **A:** Look at that beautiful building. Why don't you take a picture of it?

    B: (That's a good idea)/ Because I don't want to __.__

3 SUGGESTIONS

Look at the tourist information. Complete the conversation. Use the suggestions in the pamphlet.

BOSTON Highlights

Here are some of the many things you can do in this "capital of New England":

☑ **Go to Haymarket**—open-air fruit and vegetable stands (Fridays and Saturdays only).

☑ **Visit Faneuil Hall Marketplace**—restoration of Boston's historic Quincy Market. Shops, restaurants.

☑ **Go to The New England Aquarium**—412 species, 7,606 specimens.

☑ **Walk along the waterfront**—offices, shops, parks for picnics.

☑ **Take the "T"**—Boston's subway system.

☑ **Take a boat excursion**—cruise the harbor and Massachusetts Bay ($1\frac{1}{2}$ hours).

❑ **Go shopping in Downtown Crossing**—Boston's pedestrian zone.

❑ **Take an elevator to the top of the John Hancock Observatory**—the tallest building in New England.

❑ **Walk the Freedom Trail**—$1\frac{1}{2}$ miles of historic points of interest.

❑ **Eat at Legal Seafoods**—restaurant chain famous for fresh fish at reasonable prices. (No reservations accepted.)

A: Wow, there's so much to do! I don't know where to begin!

B: Why don't we ____visit Faneuil Hall Marketplace____? We can have breakfast there and then

              1.
do some shopping.

A: Sounds good. How will we get there?

B: Let's ____Take the "T" Boston's subway system____. I always like to see what the public

          2.
transportation is like.

(continued on next page)

A: OK. After Faneuil Hall, maybe we could ___go to Haymarket Hancock observatory___ and pick up
3.
some fresh fruit for later on. It's right across from there.

B: We can't. It's only open Fridays and Saturdays.

A: Oh, too bad. How about ___going to the John___? We could get a "bird's-eye"
4.
view of the city that way.

B: I don't know. I'm a little afraid of heights. But I've got another idea. Why don't we
___take a boat excursion___? That way we could still see a lot of the city.
5.

A: Fine. It'll be nice being on the water. And afterwards, how about
___going to the New England Aquarium___? I hear they have the largest glass-enclosed saltwater
6.
tank in the world.

B: Speaking of fish, why don't we ___eat at legal seafoods___ tonight?
7.

A: OK. But we'll have to go early if we don't want to wait. They don't take reservations.

B: That's no problem.

A: So we've decided what to do for breakfast and dinner. What about lunch?

B: Maybe we could ___walk along the waterfront___ and have a picnic in the park. And
8.
then, how about ___going shopping in Downtown Crossing___? I need to buy some souvenirs, and
9.
we won't have to worry about traffic. It's a pedestrian zone.

A: I don't know. Why don't we ___walk the Freedom Trail___? I'd really like to see some
10.
more historic sights. We can look for souvenirs tomorrow.

4 PERSONALIZATION

*Imagine you are in Boston. Look at the flier in Exercise 3. Complete
these suggestions to a friend.*

1. Why don't we _____

2. How about _____

3. Let's _____

4. Maybe we could _____

5. But let's not _____

UNIT

16

PRESENT PERFECT: SINCE AND FOR

① SPELLING: REGULAR AND IRREGULAR VERBS

Write the past participles.

Base Form	Simple Past	Past Participle
1. be	was/were	been
2. look	looked	looked.
3. come	came	come
4. bring	brought	brought
5. play	played	played
6. have	had	had
7. get	got	gotten
8. fall	fell	fallen
9. watch	watched	watched
10. lose	lost	lost
11. win	won	won
12. eat	ate	eaten

② SINCE OR FOR

Put these time expressions in the correct column.

~~1993~~	4:00 P.M.	Monday	a day	yesterday
an hour	she was a child	a long time	ten years	many months

Since	For
1993	an hour
4 PM	she was a child
Monday	a long time
Yesterday	Ten years
a day	many months

3 **AFFIRMATIVE STATEMENTS WITH *SINCE* AND *FOR***

*Complete these brief biographies of two people who have been famous since they were children. Use the present perfect form of the verbs in parentheses ( ) and choose between **since** and **for**.*

1. Tiger Woods (1976–   ) When Tiger Woods was only eighteen

months old, his father gave him a sawed-off golf club. Woods

_____has loved_____ the game of golf
          1. (love)

_____Since_____ then. As a teenager, he won
        2. (since / for)

many amateur titles. At sixteen he was the youngest person to

play in a professional golf tournament.

_____Since_____ then he _____has gone on_____ to win many
        3. (Since / For)   4. (go on)

major tournaments and to break many records. _____For_____ the past
                                                    5. (Since / For)

few years, TV viewers _____have seen_____ him in many commercials.
                           6. (see)

_____Since_____ he turned professional, Woods
        7. (Since / For)

_____has earned_____ more money and _____has broken_____
        8. (earn)   9. (break)

more records at a younger age than any other golfer.

2. Jodie Foster (1962–   ) Jodie Foster

_____has been_____ an actress
        1. (be)

_____for_____ most of her life. At the age of
      2. (since / for)

three, she began appearing in television commercials. She made

her first movie in 1972 and _____has appeared_____ in
                                  3. (appear)

dozens of movies _____Since_____ then. In
                      4. (since / for)

1985, she graduated with honors from Yale University. _____Since_____
                                                            5. (Since / For)

her graduation, she _____has received_____ two Oscars for Best Actress, for her
                         6. (receive)

roles in *The Accused* and *The Silence of the Lambs*, she _____has directed_____
                                                                  7. (direct)

her first film, *Little Man Tate*, and she _____has formed_____ her own
                                                 8. (form)

production company. _____Since_____ 1998, Foster
                         9. (Since / For)

_____has taken on_____ a new role—that of a mother to son Charles, born on
        10. (take on)

July 20.

4 QUESTIONS AND ANSWERS

Ask and answer questions about the people in Exercise 3.

Biography 1

1. How long / Tiger Woods / love golf?

  A: How long has Tiger Woods loved golf?

  B: He has loved golf since he was eighteen months old.

OR

  He has loved golf for more than twenty years.

2. How long / he / be a professional golfer?

  A: How long has he been a professional golfer?

  B: He has been a professional golfer for ~~eighteen~~ ten years.

3. he / win any major tournaments since he turned professional?

  A: Had he won any major tournaments since he turned professional

  B: He has won many.

4. How long / he / be in TV commercials?

  A: How long has he been in tv commercials.

  B: He has been in ~~a~~ commercial.

Biography 2

5. How long / Jodie Foster / be an actress?

  A: How long has Jodie Foster been an actress!

  B: Jodie Foster has been an actres for 38 years.

6. she / win any Oscars since 1985?

  A: Has she won any Oscars since 1985.

  B: she ~~xxx~~ has won two Oscars.

7. she / direct any movies since she graduated from Yale?

  A: Has she directed any movies since she graduated from Yale?

  B: she has directed

8. How long / she / be a mother?

  A: How long has she been a mother?

  B: She has been a mother for five years

⑤ AFFIRMATIVE AND NEGATIVE STATEMENTS

Read the pairs of sentences (a. and b.). Write a summary sentence that has a meaning similar to the two sentences.

1. a. Carlos became a tennis player in 1979.

   b. He is still a tennis player.

   SUMMARY: *Carlos has been a tennis player since 1979.*

2. a. Fei-Mei and Natasha competed in 1992.

   b. That was the last time they competed.

   SUMMARY: *Fei-Mei and Natasha haven't competed since 1992.*

3. a. Min Ho won two awards in 1998.

   b. He won another award in 1999.

   SUMMARY: _Min Ho has won three awards_ since 1997.

4. a. Marilyn appeared in a movie in 1998.

   b. She appeared in another movie last year.

   SUMMARY: _Marilyn has appeared in two movies_ since 1997.

5. a. Victor and Marilyn saw each other in 1998.

   b. That was the last time they saw each other.

   SUMMARY: _Victor and Marilyn haven't seen each other since 1998_

6. a. Andreas lost two games in February of this year.

   b. He lost another game last week.

   SUMMARY: _Andreas has lost three games_ since February of this year.

7. a. Tanya and Boris became skaters in 1998.

   b. They are still skaters.

   SUMMARY: _Tanya and Boris have been skaters_ since 1998.

PRESENT PERFECT:
ALREADY AND YET

---

1 SPELLING: REGULAR AND IRREGULAR VERBS

Write the past participles.

Base Form	Simple Past	Past Participle
1. become	became	become
2. act	acted	_____
3. give	gave	_____
4. keep	kept	_____
5. hold	held	_____
6. travel	traveled	_____
7. sing	sang	_____
8. dance	danced	_____
9. fight	fought	_____
10. know	knew	_____
11. drink	drank	_____
12. smile	smiled	_____

2 QUESTIONS AND STATEMENTS WITH *ALREADY* AND *YET*

Complete these conversations with the correct form of the verbs in parentheses and **already** *or* **yet**.

1. **A:** _____Have_____ you _____read_____ the paper _____yet_____?
   (read)

   B: No. I _____ time _____.
   (have)

2. **A:** They expect a lot of cases of the flu this year.

   B: I know. I _____ a vaccination. I went to
   (get)
   the doctor last week. What about you?

   A: I _____ whether I'm going to get a flu shot.
   (decide)

(continued on next page)

3. A: _____ you _____? I'm really hungry. Maybe we
    (eat)
  could get a couple of slices of pizza.

  B: Sorry. I'd like to, but I _____ dinner.
    (have)

❸ QUESTIONS AND STATEMENTS WITH *ALREADY* AND *YET*

*Monica Clarke is a home health aide. Read her list of things to do. She has
checked (✓) all the things she's already done. Ask and answer questions about the
words in parentheses ( ).*

```
              Monday, March 29

  ☑  make breakfast for pt.
  ❑  make lunch for pt.
  ☑  take pt.'s temperature
  ❑  give pt. a bath
  ☑  change pt.'s bandages
  ☑  go food shopping
  ❑  do the laundry
  ❑  call doctor for the blood-test results
  ❑  exercise pt.'s legs
  ☑  give pt. medication
```

1. (breakfast) <u>Has she made breakfast for the patient yet?</u>

   <u>She's already made breakfast for the patient.</u>

2. (lunch) <u>Has she made lunch for the patient yet?</u>

   <u>She hasn't made lunch for the patient yet.</u>

3. (food shopping) _____

   _____

4. (medication) _____

   _____

5. (doctor) _____

   _____

6. (bandages) _____

_____

7. (bath) _____

_____

8. (temperature) _____

_____

9. (laundry) _____

_____

10. (legs) _____

_____

4 EDITING

Read Monica's letter to a friend. Find and correct five mistakes in the use of the present perfect with **already** *and* **yet**. *The first mistake is already corrected.*

Dear Suzanne,

    It's 8:00 P.M. and I'm exhausted. I'm at my new job. I've already ~~work~~ worked here for two weeks. The job is hard, but I feel that the patient have already made progress. She hasn't walked already, but she's already sat up by herself. She can feed herself now, too. Already she has gained three pounds.

    How are you? When are you coming to visit? Have you decide yet? Please write.

Love,

Monica

UNIT

PRESENT PERFECT: INDEFINITE PAST

1 SPELLING: REGULAR AND IRREGULAR VERBS

Write the past participle.

Base Form	Simple Past	Past Participle
1. work	worked	worked
2. begin	began	begun
3. forgive	forgave	forgiven
4. promise	promised	promised
5. go	went	~~went~~ gone
6. feel	felt	felt
7. grow	grew	grown
8. hear	heard	heard
9. see	saw	seen
10. decide	decided	decided
11. keep	kept	kept
12. act	acted	acted

2 AFFIRMATIVE STATEMENTS

Complete these statements. Use the present perfect form of the correct verbs from Exercise 1.

1. Juliana _____ has worked _____ very hard this year.

2. She _____ has acted _____ in two Hollywood movies.

3. We _____ have seen _____ her face on many magazine covers.

4. People _____ have begun _____ to recognize her on the street.

5. I _____ have felt _____ that she is going to star in a new movie.

6. I _____ have _____ always _____ heard _____ that she's a

great actress.

80

7. Even though she is famous, she ___has kept___ her life very private.

8. Juliana ___has promised___ the press, however, to give an interview if she wins an

Oscar.

③ AFFIRMATIVE AND NEGATIVE STATEMENTS

Every year Hollywood gives out awards for movie achievements. Complete this editorial about the Academy Awards. Use the present perfect form of the verbs in parentheses ( ).

It's Oscar night once again. You and a billion other people from ninety countries around the

world ___have___ just ___turned on___ your TVs to see who Hollywood will honor
1. (turn on)
this year. The Academy of Motion Picture Arts and Sciences ___have chosen___ nominees to
2. (choose)
compete in categories including Best Picture, Best Actor, Best Actress, and Best Director. Actors

and actresses from around the world ___have come___ to Hollywood to take part in the gala
3. (come)
event.

As always, opinions about the nominations ___have been___ mixed. Many groups are
4. (be)
unhappy. Lately, there ___haven't been___ many great roles for women. In fact, there
5. (not be)
___has___ seldom ___been___ a Hollywood actress who ___has worked___ past
6. (be) **7. (work)**
the age of 45. "I ___have___ recently ___read___ several scripts," said one
8. (read)
well-known actress, "and I ___have rejected___ all of them. The stories are ridiculous." This
9. (reject)
absence of good roles for women may partly explain why out of more than 2,000 Oscar awards,

fewer than 300 ___have gone___ to women.
10. (go)
African-American actors and actresses ___have___ also ___felt___ excluded.
11. (feel)
Fewer than ten ___have gotten___ awards for acting.
12. (get)
Actors and actresses with physical disabilities ___haven't gotten___ major roles either. Many
13. (not get)
movies ___have___ recently ___told___ the stories of people who are blind or
14. (tell)
paralyzed, but "able-bodied" Hollywood stars ___have played___ these parts.
15. (play)

(continued on next page)

On screen as well as off, we still have a long way to go toward equal opportunity. In the meantime, Hollywood _has produced_ another evening of glitter and glamour as movies

16. (produce)

continue to fascinate and entertain us. As one actor said, "They take us to places we

have never _been_ and allow us to see things we _have_

17. (be)

never _seen_ ."

18. (see)

So, relax, have some popcorn, and enjoy the show.

4 QUESTIONS

Bob Waters is interviewing a movie star. Read the star's answers. Write Bob's questions.

1. **BOB:** _How many movies have you been in?_

   STAR: I've been in ten movies.

2. **BOB:** _____

   STAR: I've received four nominations for Best Actor.

3. **BOB:** Some actors don't like to see their own films.

   _____

   STAR: No, I haven't. I've never watched the completed films.

4. **BOB:** _____

   STAR: No, never. I've never gone to the Academy Awards. I prefer to watch the event on

   TV.

5. **BOB:** Your last movie was an Italian production.

   _____

   STAR: I've acted in foreign films three times.

6. **BOB:** _____

    STAR: Yes, I have. I worked with Sophia Loren once.

7. **BOB:** _____

    STAR: No. I've never been in a French film.

8. **BOB:** You've made a lot of money in a very short time.

    _____

    STAR: How? It's changed my life in many ways. I've traveled more, I've bought a new

        house . , ,

9. **BOB:** _____

    STAR: No, I haven't. I haven't read any good scripts lately. But I'm sure a good one will

        come my way soon.

❺ PERSONALIZATION

Write about your own experience going to the movies, renting a video, or watching TV.

1. _____ recently _____.

2. _____ lately.

3. _____ never _____.

4. _____ just _____.

PRESENT PERFECT AND
SIMPLE PAST TENSE

  1 PRESENT PERFECT OR SIMPLE PAST TENSE

Complete the chart about Joe Dorsey, a teacher who is looking for a job.

	Last Year	**This Year**
1.	Joe answered twenty employment ads.	*Joe has answered* thirty ads.
2.	*Joe had* two job interviews.	Joe has had three job interviews.
3.	*Joe got* one job offer.	Joe has gotten three job offers.
4.	Joe made $24,000.	*Joe has made* the same amount of money.
5.	Joe was sick once.	*Joe has been* sick twice.
6.	*Joe looked* well.	Joe has looked tired.
7.	*Joe bought* a new camera.	Joe has bought a VCR.
8.	Joe paid with cash.	*Joe has paid* by credit card.
9.	Joe read five books.	*Joe has read* two books.
10.	*Joe felt* discouraged.	Joe has felt more encouraged.

❷ PRESENT PERFECT OR SIMPLE PAST TENSE

A journalist is interviewing a woman about marriage. Complete the interview with the correct form of the verbs in parentheses ( ).

INTERVIEWER: How long _____have_____ you _____been_____ married?
1. (be)

WOMAN: Let's see. We _____got_____ married in 1997, so we __have been__
2. (get) **3. (be)**
married for just a few years.

INTERVIEWER: And when _____Did_____ you _____have_____ your first child?
4. (have)

WOMAN: Well, I __became__ a mother pretty quickly. We ~~have~~ had
5. (become) **6. (have)**
Stephanie ten months after we __had been__ married.
7. (be)

INTERVIEWER: You say this isn't your first marriage. How long __did__ your first
marriage __last__ ?
8. (last)

WOMAN: About two years. We __divorced__ in 1989.
9. (divorce)

INTERVIEWER: __Did__ you __have__ any kids?
10. (have)

WOMAN: No, we __did__.
11.

INTERVIEWER: Do you still see your first husband?

WOMAN: Yes. We __remaind__ friends. In fact, I __have saw__ him last week.
12. (remain) **13. (see)**
He and Joe __have become__ friends, too.
14. (become)

INTERVIEWER: __Did__ he __remarry__ ?
15. (remarry)

WOMAN: No, he __did__.
16.

INTERVIEWER: In your opinion, why __did__ your first marriage __fail__ ?
17. (fail)

WOMAN: I think that we __got__ married too young. We __didn't know__
18. (get) **19. (not know)**
each other well enough.

INTERVIEWER: Where __did__ you __meet__ Joe?
20. (meet)

WOMAN: In Atlanta. We __were__ both students there.
21. (be)

INTERVIEWER: And when __did__ you __move__ to Los Angeles?
22. (move)

WOMAN: This year. Los Angeles is the third city we __have lived__ in! Joe teaches
23. (live)
college, and it's hard to find a permanent job these days.

❸ PRESENT PERFECT OR SIMPLE PAST TENSE

Read some facts about the changing American family. Complete the statements.
Use the correct form of the verbs in the boxes.

begin	change	get	have

The American family ___has changed___ a lot in the past forty years. In the 1960s,

couples ___began___ to get married at an older age. They also ___~~began~~ got___
     2.   **3.**

divorced more frequently than they ever did, and they ___had___ fewer children.
                                                                 4.

be	create	occur	rise

Age

In 1960, the average age for marriage for women ___was___ 20.3 and for men,
                                                         5.

22.8. Today it ___has risen___ to 25.0 for women and 26.8 for men. In the early 1960s,
            6.

most divorces ___occur___ among couples older than 45. Today people of all ages are
                      7.

getting divorced at a very high rate. This, in part, ___has created___ many single-parent
                                                         8.

homes.

be	begin	have	increase

Birth Rate

In the mid-1960s, birth rates ___began___ to drop. Then, almost 60 percent of
                                9.

women ___had___ three or more children by the time they ___were___ in their
          10.   **11.**

late thirties. These days, 35 percent of women in the same age group have only two

children. In addition, the number of births to older women ___has___ greatly

___increased___.
     12.

change	get	reach	stay

Living Arrangements

Before 1960, most children ___~~got~~ stayed___ in their parents' homes until they
                                              13.

___get___ married. This pattern ___has changed___ since then. Today many single
     14.   **15.**

people live alone. Also affecting living arrangements is the fact that life expectancy

___has reached___ an all-time high of 76.5 years. This means that there are a lot more older
     16.

people, and some of them are moving in with their adult children.

4 EDITING

Read this student's letter to a friend. Find and correct eight mistakes in the use of the present perfect and the simple past tense. The first mistake is already corrected.

Dear Jennifer,

    Last month, I ~~have~~ **met** the most wonderful guy. His name is Roger, and he is a student in my night class. He **has** lived here since 1992. Before that he **had** lived in Detroit too, so we have a lot in common. Roger ~~has been~~ **was** married for five years but got divorced last April.

    Roger and I ~~spent~~ **spend** a lot of time together. Last week I saw him every night, and this week we've already gotten together three times after class. Monday night we ~~have seen~~ **saw** a great movie. ~~Did you see~~ **Have you seen** *The Purple Room?* It's playing at all the theaters.

    We decided to take a trip back to Detroit in the summer. Maybe we can get together! It would be great to see you again. Please let me know if you'll be there.

Love,

Diana

P.S. I'm enclosing a photo of Roger that I've ~~taken~~ **took** a few weeks ago.

PRESENT PERFECT PROGRESSIVE

❶ AFFIRMATIVE STATEMENTS WITH *SINCE* AND *FOR*

Read the information about a married couple, Pete and Amanda Kelly. Write a sentence that summarizes the information.

1. The year is 2000. Pete and Amanda Kelly moved to New York in 1997. They are still living there.

   They have been living in New York since 1997 OR for three years.

2. Amanda began work at the *Daily News* in 1999. She's still working there.

   _____

3. Amanda is writing articles about the homeless. She began a series last month.

   _____

4. The number of homeless Americans is increasing. It began to increase steadily in 1980.

   _____

5. Pete is working at a homeless shelter. He started last month.

   _____

6. Pete went back to school last year. He's studying economics.

   _____

7. Amanda and Pete started looking for a new apartment two months ago. They are still looking.

   _____

❷ AFFIRMATIVE AND NEGATIVE STATEMENTS

Complete the statements. Use the present perfect progressive form of the verbs in the box.

eat	rain	run	study	wait
feel	~~rub~~	sleep	try	work

1. Amanda's eyes are red. She *'s been rubbing* _____ them all morning.

2. She's tired. She _____ well lately.

3. She's losing weight. She _____ much lately.

4. Pete is exhausted too. He _____ all night for a test.

5. Amanda doesn't know many people at the *Daily News*. She

   _____ there very long.

6. She just looked out the window. The street is wet. It _____.

7. Pete is out of breath. He _____.

8. He's only five minutes late. Amanda _____ very long.

9. They're going to look at an apartment. They _____ to find

   one for months.

10. It's very hard to find an apartment in New York. They're often too expensive. Amanda

    and Pete _____ very hopeful.

❸ PERSONALIZATION

What have or haven't you been doing? Complete these statements with information about yourself. Use the present perfect progressive.

1. _____ all year.

2. _____ lately.

3. _____ since 2000.

4. _____ for the last half hour.

5. _____

4 QUESTIONS WITH *HOW LONG*

Look at the picture. Ask questions about the man on the bench, the woman with the dog, the children, the police officer, the two men, and the weather. Begin with **How long** *and use the present perfect progressive.*

1. <u>How long has the man been sitting</u> _____ on the bench?

2. _____ under the tree?

3. _____ the dog?

4. _____ ball?

5. _____ it _____?

6. _____ the bus?

PRESENT PERFECT AND PRESENT PERFECT PROGRESSIVE

1 PRESENT PERFECT OR PRESENT PERFECT PROGRESSIVE

Read this information about a famous British businesswoman and environmentalist. Complete it with the present perfect or present perfect progressive form of the verbs in parentheses ( ). If either form is possible, use the present perfect progressive.

In a short period of time, Anita Roddick

_____ has become _____ one of the most
    1. (become)
successful businesswomen in the world. She is

the owner of an international chain of stores

that sells soaps, makeup, body lotions, and

creams. For more than twenty years, The Body

Shop _____ products that are
    2. (sell)
"environmentally friendly." They are made mostly of natural products

from renewable sources, and they come in biodegradable, recyclable

containers. In addition, Roddick, who _____ for years
                                    3. (fight)
against the practice of animal testing of cosmetics, refuses to use any

animals in the testing of her products.

The first Body Shop opened in Brighton, England, in 1976. Since then,

more than 1,500 stores in more than forty-five countries around the world

_____. Roddick relies on the reputation of her products
    4. (open)
and stores to attract customers. She _____ never

_____ much advertising for her stores. Lately, however,
    5. (do)

(continued on next page)

you *will* see Roddick's face if you turn on your TV. She _____ on

6. (appear)

commercials for the American Express charge card.

Roddick spends almost half of her time traveling. Right now she is "on the road." For

the past several months, she _____ around the world in search of new

7. (travel)

ideas for her body-care products.

Roddick is more than a businesswoman. She _____ several awards,

8. (receive)

including the United Nations Global 500 environmental award. She is also concerned with

human rights, and she _____ a London newspaper that is sold by

9. (start)

homeless people.

Roddick _____ an autobiography called *Body and Soul: Profits with*

10. (write)

Principles. Published in 1991, the book shows how Roddick _____

successfully _____ business with social responsibility.

11. (combine)

❷ PRESENT PERFECT OR PRESENT PERFECT PROGRESSIVE

*Complete this conversation between two friends. Use the present perfect or present
perfect progressive form of the verbs in parentheses ( ).*

A: Hi. I _____ haven't seen _____ you around lately. How

1. (not see)

_____ you _____?

2. (be)

B: OK, thanks. What about you?

A: Not bad. What _____ you _____?

3. (do)

B: Nothing special. What about you?

A: I _____ a book for this business course I'm taking. It's called

4. (read)

Body and Soul. It's pretty interesting. I can lend it to you when I'm done, if you'd like.

B: Who's it by?

A: Anita Roddick. _____ you ever _____ anything

5. (read)

about her?

B: Yes. I _____ a few articles about her in the paper.

6. (see)

A: _____ you ever _____ any of her
7. (buy)

products?

B: As a matter of fact, I _____ her products for years.
8. (use)

A: Oh. Where do you buy them?

B: A new shop _____ just _____ on
9. (open)

Broadway.

A: Wow, they _____ everywhere, haven't they? I wonder where
10. (open)

the next one is going to be.

3 QUESTIONS: PRESENT PERFECT OR PRESENT PERFECT PROGRESSIVE

Use the cues to write questions about Anita Roddick.

1. she / sell / cosmetics for a long time?

   Has she been selling cosmetics for a long time?

2. How much money / her business / make this year?

   _____

3. How long / she / travel around the world?

   _____

4. How many countries / she / visit?

   _____

5. How many copies of her book / she / sell?

   _____

6. she / write / any books since *Body and Soul*?

   _____

7. she / ever appear on TV?

   _____

8. How long / she and her husband / live in England?

   _____

4 EDITING

Read this student's journal entry. Find and correct seven mistakes in the use of the present perfect and present perfect progressive. The first mistake is already corrected.

Friday, Sept. 15

It's the second week of the fall semester. I've ~~taken~~ **been taking** *a business course with Professor McCarthy. For the past two weeks we've studying people who have been becoming very successful in the world of business. As part of the course, we've been reading books by or about internationally famous businesspeople. For example, I've just been finishing a book by Bill Gates, the CEO of Microsoft, called* <u>Business @ The Speed of Thought</u>. *It was fascinating. Since then I've read* <u>Body and Soul</u> *by Anita Roddick, the owner of The Body Shop. I've only been reading about fifty pages of the book so far, but it seems interesting. Although I bought her products ever since one of her stores opened in my neighborhood, I really didn't know much about her.*

ANSWER KEY

Where the full form is given, the contraction is also acceptable. Where the contracted form is given, the full form is also acceptable.

PART | **PRESENT, PAST, AND FUTURE: REVIEW AND EXPANSION**

UNIT **PRESENT PROGRESSIVE AND SIMPLE PRESENT TENSE**

2. getting, gets
3. trying, tries
4. planning, plans
5. having, has
6. doing, does
7. matching, matches
8. grabbing, grabs
9. giving, gives
10. saying, says

2

2. drives
3. takes
4. isn't taking
5. is taking
6. are repairing
7. is using
8. doesn't . . . use
9. takes
10. moves
11. is slowing down
12. 's raining
13. doesn't like
14. drives
15. is listening
16. listens
17. is describing
18. doesn't want
19. isn't moving
20. hates
21. feels
22. knows
23. wishes

3

(Answers will vary.)

4

Postcard 1
2. is shining
3. is blowing
4. feels
5. know
6. are flying
7. are building
Postcard 2
1. are traveling
2. 'm standing
3. is getting
4. looks
5. has
6. 's taking
7. 's starting
Postcard 3
1. 'm studying
2. living
3. is improving
4. speak
5. 're helping
6. want
7. miss

5

3. Mario and Silvia OR They go to school.
4. Mario and Silvia OR They are having lunch.
5. Mario studies at the library. Silvia plays basketball.
6. Mario goes home. Silvia visits her grandmother.
7. Mario and Silvia OR They are doing (their) homework.
8. Mario has dinner. Silvia practices the guitar.
9. Mario plays computer games. Silvia makes dinner.
10. Mario is reading the newspaper. Silvia is washing the dishes.

6

2. He doesn't listen to the radio. He watches TV.
3. Silvia doesn't visit her grandfather. She visits her grandmother.
4. She isn't practicing the piano. She's practicing the guitar.
5. He doesn't watch the news. He reads the newspaper.

7

2. **A:** When do Mario and Silvia get up?
   B: They get up at 7:30.
3. **A:** Does Silvia watch TV in the morning?
   B: No, she doesn't.
4. **A:** What are they doing now?
   B: They're having lunch.
5. **A:** Is Mario studying at the library now?
   B: No, he isn't.
6. **A:** Does he do his homework at school?
   B: No, he doesn't.
7. **A:** When does Silvia play basketball?
   B: She plays basketball at 3:00.
8. **A:** Does Mario play computer games before dinner?
   B: No, he doesn't.

8

2. Silvia is usually on time.
3. Silvia and Mario never miss school.
4. These days they're studying English. OR They're studying English these days.
5. They usually speak Italian.
6. Now they're speaking English. OR They're speaking English now.
7. Silvia and Mario always do their homework.
8. Mario is often tired.
9. The students usually eat lunch in school.
10. They're always hungry.
11. At the moment Silvia is having a snack. OR Silvia is having a snack at the moment.
12. Silvia rarely goes to bed late.

9

Hi, How are you? I ~~write~~ **'m writing** you this letter on the bus. I hope you can read my writing. They ~~do~~ **'re doing** some repairs on the road, so it's bumpy and the bus ~~shakes~~ **is shaking**. Guess what? I ~~am having~~ **have** a job as a clerk in the mail room of a small company. The pay isn't good, but I ~~'m liking~~ **I like** the people there. They're all friendly, and we ~~are speaking~~ **speak** Spanish all the time. I'm also taking Spanish classes at night at a language institute. The class ~~is meeting~~ **meets**

three times a week. It just started last week, so ~~I'm not knowing~~ **I don't know** many of the other students yet. They seem nice, though.

~~I'm thinking~~ **I think** that I'm beginning to get accustomed to living here. At first I experienced some "culture shock." I understand that this is quite normal. But these days I ~~meet~~ **'m meeting** more and more people because of my job and my class, so I'm feeling more connected to things.

What ~~do you do~~ **are you doing** these days? ~~Do you still look~~ **Are you still looking** for a new job?

Please write when you can. I always like to hear from you.

UNIT 2 IMPERATIVE

1

2. Look down.
3. Don't lean backward.
4. Take a small step.
5. Don't breathe in.
6. Count slowly.
7. Don't speak loudly.
8. Keep your eyes shut.
9. Don't wear tight clothes.
10. Wear light clothes.
11. Don't turn the lights off.
12. Turn the music up.
13. Put the heat on low.
14. Don't come late.

2

3.	Walk	9.	stop
4.	ride	10.	Don't cross
5.	Go	11.	be
6.	Don't turn	12.	Don't pass
7.	make	13.	Have
8.	Continue	14.	Don't work

3

Your mother called. ~~Calls~~ **Call** her at your sister's tonight.

Don't ~~you~~ call after 10:00, though.

I went to the gym.

Please *
~~Wash please~~ the dishes and ~~threw~~ out the trash. **throw**

If anyone calls for me, ~~takes~~ a message. **take**

Thanks a lot.

* OTHER POSSIBLE CORRECTIONS: Wash the dishes, please, and throw out the trash. OR Wash the dishes and throw out the trash, please.

4

(Answers will vary.)

UNIT **3** SIMPLE PAST TENSE

1

3. caught	15. needed
4. did	16. opened
5. looked	17. put
6. found	18. read
7. gave	19. said
8. hurried	20. thought
9. saw	21. understood
10. died	22. voted
11. kissed	23. won
12. came	24. felt
13. lived	25. was . . . were
14. met	

2

2. was	7. wasn't . . . was
3. weren't . . . were	8. was . . . wasn't
4. wasn't	9. were
5. was	10. were
6. wasn't . . . was	

3

2. **A:** Where was Simone de Beauvoir from?
   B: She was from France.
3. **A:** What nationality was Pablo Neruda?
   B: He was Chilean.
4. **A:** Who was Boccaccio?
   B: He was a poet and storyteller.
5. **A:** Was Agatha Christie French?
   B: No, she wasn't.
6. **A:** What nationality was Lorraine Hansberry?
   B: She was American.
7. **A:** Was Honoré de Balzac a poet?
   B: No, he wasn't.
8. **A:** When was Karel Čapek born?
   B: He was born in 1890.
9. **A:** Who was Isaak Babel?
   B: He was a short-story writer and playwright.

4

Biography 1
2. spent
3. wrote
4. included
5. translated
6. died

Biography 2
1. was
2. lived
3. began
4. called
5. had
6. painted

Biography 3
1. were
2. built
3. flew
4. watched
5. took place
6. lasted

5

2. **A:** What did he do?
   B: He was a writer. OR He wrote books and translated other people's works.
3. **A:** Did he write poetry?
   B: No, he didn't.
4. **A:** Where did he spend most of his life?
   B: (He spent most of his life) in the United States.
5. **A:** What did people call Anna Mary Robertson Moses?
   B: (They called her) Grandma Moses.
6. **A:** What did she do?
   B: She was a painter. OR She painted.
7. **A:** When did she begin painting?
   B: She began painting in her seventies.
8. **A:** Did she have formal art training?
   B: No, she didn't.
9. **A:** Where did the Wright brothers build their first planes?
   B: (They built their first planes) in their bicycle shop in Ohio.
10. **A:** Did both brothers fly the *Flyer 1*?
    B: No, they didn't.
11. **A:** Where did the first controlled flight take place?
    B: (It took place) near Kitty Hawk, North Carolina.
12. **A:** How long did the flight last?
    B: (It lasted) only about 12 seconds.

6

3. Orville didn't have serious health problems.
4. Wilbur didn't grow a moustache.
5. Orville didn't lose most of his hair.
6. Wilbur didn't take courses in Latin.

7. Wilbur didn't like to play jokes.
8. Wilbur didn't dress very fashionably.
9. Wilbur didn't play the guitar.
10. Orville didn't build the first glider.
11. Orville didn't make the first attempts to fly.
12. Orville didn't choose the location of Kitty Hawk.
13. Wilbur didn't have a lot of patience.
14. Wilbur didn't live a long life.

7

Pablo Neruda (1904–1973) Pablo Neruda ~~were~~ **was** a famous poet, political activist, and diplomat. He was born in Parral, Chile. When he was seventeen, he ~~gone~~ **went** to Santiago to continue his education. He did not ~~finished~~ **finish**, but he soon published his first book. Neruda ~~spends~~ **spent** the next several decades traveling and continuing to write poetry. In 1971, while he was Chile's ambassador to France, he ~~winned~~ **won** the Nobel Prize in literature. He ~~dead~~ **died** two years later.

UNIT 4 USED TO

1

2. People used to read
3. People used to cook
4. People used to fly
5. People used to have
6. People used to wash
7. People used to use
8. It used to take

2

2. didn't use to work
3. didn't use to have
4. used to take
5. didn't use to be
6. used to live
7. didn't use to like
8. didn't use to know
9. used to return
10. used to write

3

2. **A:** Where did she use to live?
   B: She used to live in New York.

3. **A:** What did she use to do?
   B: She used to be a student.
4. **A:** Did she use to have long hair?
   B: Yes, she did.
5. **A:** Did she use to wear glasses?
   B: No, she didn't.
6. **A:** Did she use to be married?
   B: Yes, she did.
7. **A:** Did she use to use *Ms.* before her name?
   B: No, she didn't.

4

Today I ran into an old classmate. At first, I almost didn't recognize him! He looked so different. He used to ~~had~~ **have** very dark hair. Now he's almost all gray. He also used to ~~being~~ **be** a little heavy. Now he's quite thin. And he was wearing a suit and tie! I couldn't believe it. He never ~~use~~ **used** to dress that way. He only used to wear jeans! His personality seemed different, too. He didn't ~~used~~ **use** to talk very much. Now he seems very outgoing.

I wonder what he thought about me! I'm sure I look and act a lot different from the way I ~~was~~ used to too!

5

(Answers will vary.)

UNIT 5 PAST PROGRESSIVE AND SIMPLE PAST TENSE

1

2. wasn't writing
3. was answering
4. were eating
5. weren't eating
6. was attending
7. weren't writing
8. were discussing
9. wasn't answering
10. was returning

2

2. **A:** What was he doing at 9:30?
   B: He was meeting with Ms. Jacobs.
3. **A:** Was Mr. Cotter writing police reports at 10:30?
   B: No, he wasn't.

4. **A:** What kind of reports was he writing?
   B: He was writing financial reports.
5. **A:** What was he doing at 11:30?
   B: He was answering correspondence.
6. **A:** Was he having lunch at 12:00?
   B: Yes, he was.
7. **A:** Who was eating lunch with him?
   B: Mr. Webb was eating lunch with him.
8. **A:** Where were they having lunch?
   B: They were having lunch at Sol's Cafe.
9. **A:** Who was he talking to at 3:30?
   B: He was talking to Alan.
10. **A:** What were they discussing?
    B: They were discussing the budget.

❸

3. were visiting	17. arrived
4. took place	18. found
5. killed	19. was walking
6. injured	20. went off
7. took	21. had
8. exploded	22. were carrying
9. went out	23. were riding
10. stopped	24. went out
11. started	25. stopped
12. were eating	26. had to
13. shook	27. reached
14. occurred	28. was waiting
15. crumbled	29. drove
16. collapsed	30. was happening

❹

2. What happened when the bomb exploded?
3. What were the schoolchildren doing when the lights went out?
4. How many people were working in the building when the bomb exploded?
5. What were they doing when the bomb went off?
6. What happened to the offices when the blast occurred?
7. What was he doing when the bomb exploded?
8. What happened when the rescue workers brought him to the ambulance?

UNIT **FUTURE**

❶

2. She's going to wash the car.
3. They're going to get gas.
4. She's going to make a left turn.
5. She's going to get a ticket.
6. They're going to crash.
7. They're going to eat lunch.
8. It's going to rain.

2. How long are you going to stay?
3. Are you going to stay at a hotel?
4. What are you going to do in San Francisco?
5. Are you going to visit Fisherman's Wharf?
6. Is your daughter going to go with you?
7. What is he going to do?
8. When are you going to leave?

2. He isn't going to take the train. He's going to fly OR take a plane.
3. He isn't going to travel alone. He's going to travel with his wife.
4. They aren't going to leave from Chicago. They're going to leave from New York.
5. They aren't going to fly US Airways. They're going to fly FairAirs.
6. They aren't going to leave on July 11. They're going to leave on June 11.
7. It isn't going to depart at 7:00 A.M. It's going to depart at 7:00 P.M.
8. They aren't going to sit apart. They're going to sit together.
9. They aren't going to be in a smoking section. They're going to be in a non-smoking OR no smoking section.
10. She isn't going to sit in seat 15B. She's going to sit in seat 15C.

2. will	16. will
3. will become	17. will . . . help
4. Will . . . replace	18. won't replace
5. won't replace	19. 'll perform
6. will . . . operate	20. won't be
7. will . . . do	21. will improve
8. 'll be	22. will lose
9. 'll sing	23. will create
10. 'll dance	24. Will . . . need
11. Will . . . tell	25. will . . . look
12. will	26. won't look
13. won't . . . be	27. 'll resemble
14. will . . . do	28. will . . . happen
15. Will . . . have	29. 'll happen

Next Wednesday <u>is</u> the first performance of *Bats*. Melissa Robins <u>is playing</u> the leading role. Robins, who lives in Italy and who is vacationing in Greece, is not available for an interview at this time. She <u>is</u>, however, <u>appearing</u> on Channel 8's "Theater Talk" sometime next month.

Although shows traditionally begin at 8:00 P.M., *Bats*, because of its length, <u>starts</u> a half hour earlier.

Immediately following the opening-night performance, the company <u>is having</u> a reception in the theater lounge. Tickets are still available. Call 555-6310 for more information.

6

2. I'm going to do
3. I'll ask
4. it's going to rain
5. are they showing
6. we're going to have
7. I'll take
8. We're going to arrive
9. are we going to get
10. We'll take
11. We're landing
12. are you going to stay

7

'm
I going to stay here for a week with my parents.

We have a lot of fun things planned.
we're seeing OR we're going to see
Tomorrow night we'll see a play called *Bats*. Mom

already bought tickets for it. The play begins at
're having OR we're going to have
8:00, and before that we have dinner on

Fisherman's Wharf. Right now we're sitting in

Golden Gate Park, but we have to leave. It has
's going to
suddenly gotten very cloudy. It will rain!
'll call
I call you soon.

Jason

UNIT 7 FUTURE TIME CLAUSES

1

2. is . . . 'll drink (c)
3. finish . . . 'll do (g)
4. washes . . . 'll dry (e)
5. get in . . . 'll fasten (d)
6. gets . . . 'll drive (b)
7. stops . . . 'll need (f)
8. is . . . 'll be (a)

2

2. will apply . . . before . . . finishes
3. After . . . finishes . . . 'll visit
4. While . . . works . . . 'll take
5. 'll visit . . . before . . . gets
6. When . . . finishes . . . 'll fly
7. 'll get married . . . when . . . 's
8. 'll return . . . after . . . gets married

3

2. retire
3. will . . . go
4. have
5. turn
6. will want
7. visit
8. won't want

4

2. Vera saves enough money from her summer job, she's going to buy a plane ticket.
3. Vera goes home, she's going to buy presents for her family.
4. Vera arrives at the airport, her father will be there to drive her home.
5. Vera and her father get home, they'll have dinner.
6. Vera will give her family the presents . . . they finish dinner.
7. Vera's brother will wash the dishes . . . Vera's sister dries them.
8. The whole family will stay up talking . . . the clock strikes midnight.
9. they go to bed, they'll all feel very tired.
10. Vera will fall asleep . . . her head hits the pillow.

5

(Answers will vary.)

UNIT 8 WH- QUESTIONS: SUBJECT AND PREDICATE

1

2. Whose phone rang at midnight?
3. Who was calling for Michelle?
4. Who was having a party?
5. How many people left the party?
6. What surprised them?
7. Whose friend called the police?
8. How many police arrived?
9. What happened next?
10. Who told the police about a theft?
11. Whose jewelry disappeared?
12. How many necklaces vanished?

2

2. How many rooms does her apartment have? (f)
3. How much rent does she pay? (j)
4. When does she pay the rent? (c)
5. Who(m) does she live with? (h)
6. What does she do? (g)
7. Which company does she work for? (d)

8. How long does she plan to stay there? (a)
9. How does she get to work? (b)
10. Why does she take the bus? (i)

 3

2. Why did you leave Chicago?
3. Who moved with you?
4. Where did you get a job?
5. When did it start?
6. How many rooms does it have?
7. How many of the rooms came with carpeting?
8. How much do you each pay?
9. What do you need to buy?
10. Whose brother wants to visit her?
11. Who called last Sunday?
12. Who(m) did you speak to?
13. When do they want to visit you?
14. Why is there plenty of room?

PART ‖ PRONOUNS AND PHRASAL VERBS

UNIT **9** REFLEXIVE AND RECIPROCAL PRONOUNS

 1

2. himself
3. themselves
4. itself
5. herself
6. yourself OR yourselves (yourselves OR yourself)
7. themselves
8. itself
9. themselves
10. ourselves

2

2. each other
3. herself
4. themselves
5. each other's
6. herself
7. yourselves
8. itself
9. ourselves
10. each other

3

2. are enjoying each other's
3. is going to help himself
4. are talking to themselves
5. are introducing themselves
6. are talking to each other
7. drove herself
8. blames OR is blaming himself
9. are criticizing one another OR each other
10. are thanking one another OR each other

 4

I really enjoyed ~~me~~ *myself* at Gina's party! Hank was there and we talked to ~~ourselves~~ *each other* OR *one another* quite a bit. He's a little depressed about losing his job. He thinks it's all his own fault, and he blames ~~him~~ *himself* for the whole thing. Hank introduced ~~myself~~ *me* to several of his friends. I spoke a lot to this one woman, Cara. We have a lot of things in common, and after just an hour, we felt like we had known ~~each other's~~ *each other* forever. Cara, ~~himself~~ *herself*, is a computer programmer, just like me.

At first I was nervous about going to the party alone. I sometimes feel a little uncomfortable when I'm in a social situation by ~~oneself~~ *myself*. But this time was different. Before I went, I kept telling myself to relax. My roommate, too, kept telling ~~myself~~ *me*, "Don't be so hard on ~~you~~ *yourself*! Just have fun!" That's what I advised Hank to do, too. Before we left the party, Hank and I promised ~~us~~ *each other* OR *one another* to keep in touch. I hope to see him again soon.

UNIT **10** PHRASAL VERBS

1

2. out
3. on
4. off
5. up
6. out
7. down
8. out
9. up
10. up
11. out
12. up
13. out
14. in
15. out

2

2. Pick out, help . . . out
3. Look up
4. Set up, talk over
5. Write up
6. Look . . . over
7. Do . . . over
8. Hand . . . in

 3

2. clean it up
3. call her up
4. turn it down
5. wake him up
6. turn it down
7. hand them in
8. drop it off

4

2. Bring up the homework problems. OR Bring the homework problems up.
3. Point out common mistakes. OR Point common mistakes out.
4. Talk them over.
5. Go on to the next unit.
6. Call off Friday's class. OR Call Friday's class off.
7. Make up the final exam questions. OR Make the final exam questions up.
8. Hand them out.

5

How are things going? I'm already into the second month of the spring semester, and I've got a lot of work to do. For science class, I have to write a term paper. The professor made ~~over~~ ^up^ a list of possible topics. After looking ~~over them~~ ^them over^, I think I've picked one out. I'm going to write about chimpanzees. I've already gone to the library to look ^up^ some information about them in the ^OR up^ encyclopedia ~~up~~. I found ~~up~~ ^out^ some very interesting facts.

Did you know that their hands look very much like their feet, and that they have fingernails and toenails? Their thumbs and big toes are "opposable." This makes it easy for them to pick things ~~out~~ ^up^ with both their fingers and toes. Their arms are longer than their legs. This helps ~~out them~~ ^them out^ too, because they can reach out to fruit growing on thin branches that could not otherwise support their weight. Adult males weigh between 90 and 115 pounds, and they are about four feet high when they stand ~~out~~ ^up^.

Like humans, chimpanzees are very social. They travel in groups called "communities." Mothers bring ~~out~~ ^up^ their chimps, who stay with them until about the age of seven. Even after the chimps have grown up, there is still a lot of contact with other chimpanzees.

I could go on, but I need to stop writing now so I can clean ~~out~~ ^up^ my room (it's a mess!) a little before going to bed. It's late already, and I have to get ~~early up~~ ^up early^ tomorrow morning for my 9:00 A.M. class.

Please write and let me know how you are. Or call ~~up me~~ ^me up^ sometime! It would be great to speak to you.

PART ||| MODALS AND RELATED VERBS AND EXPRESSIONS

UNIT ||| ABILITY: *CAN, COULD, BE ABLE TO*

1

3. can read an English newspaper . . . could (read one)
4. couldn't read an English novel . . . can't (read one).
5. can speak on the phone . . . couldn't (speak on the phone).
6. couldn't speak with a group of people . . . can (speak with a group of people).
7. couldn't write a social letter . . . can (write one).
8. Before the course he couldn't write a business letter, and he still can't (write one).
9. He can order a meal in English now, and he could (order a meal in English) before, too.
10. He can go shopping now, and he could (go shopping) before, too.
SUMMARY: Fernando can do a lot more now than he could (do) before the course.

2

2. **A:** What languages can you speak?
3. **A:** Could you speak Spanish when you were a child?
   B: No, I couldn't.
4. **A:** Could you speak French?
   B: Yes, I could.
5. **A:** Before you came here, could you understand spoken English?
   B: No, I couldn't.
6. **A:** Can you understand song lyrics?
   B: Yes, I can.
7. **A:** Before this course, could you write a business letter in English?
   B: No, I couldn't.
8. **A:** Could you drive a car before you came here?
   B: No, I couldn't.
9. **A:** Can you drive a car now?
   B: No, I can't.
10. **A:** Can you swim?
    B: Yes, I can.

11. A: Could you surf before you came here?
   B: No, I couldn't.
12. A: What can you do now that you couldn't do before?
   B: can do . . . couldn't do

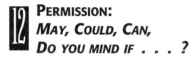

3

2. are able to interpret
3. are not able to distinguish
4. are not able to understand
5. are able to hear
6. have been able to regain
7. are able to read
8. is not able to recognize
9. is not able to work
10. are able to communicate

4

2. A: Will she be able to hear
   B: Yes, she will.
3. A: Will she be able to hear
   B: No, she won't.
4. A: Will she be able to hear
   B: Yes, she will.
5. A: Will she be able to hear
   B: Yes, she will.

5

2. could read
3. could not OR couldn't accept
4. was able to learn
5. was able to accept
6. could see
7. will . . . be able to do
8. can do
9. can do
10. has been able to master
11. has been able to speak
12. will be able to get

6

Before I came to this country I can't [couldn't] do many things in English. For example, I couldn't follow a conversation if many people were talking at the same time. I remember one occasion at a party. I wasn't able understand [to] a word! I felt so uncomfortable. Finally, my aunt came to pick me up, and I could [was able to] leave the party.

Today I can to understand much better. Since last month I can [have been able to] practice a lot. I am taking classes at the adult center. My teacher is very good. She can explains [explain] things well, and she

always gives us the chance to talk a lot in class. I can do a lot now, and I think in a few more months I can ['ll be able to] do even more.

7

(Answers will vary.)

UNIT **PERMISSION:**
MAY, COULD, CAN,
DO YOU MIND IF . . . ?

1

2. c.   **6.** a.
3. b.   **7.** e.
4. h.   **8.** g.
5. f.

2

2. we (please) review Unit 6 (please)?
3. I (please) borrow your pen (please)?
4. I look at your (class) notes?
5. I come late to the next class?
6. my husband (please) come to the next class with me (please)?
7. I (please) ask a question (please)?
8. we (please) use a dictionary (please)?
9. we (please) leave five minutes early (please)?
10. my sister goes on the class trip with the rest of the class?

3

(Answers will vary.)

4

2. can bring   **6.** may not pay
3. can't OR cannot drink **7.** may not purchase
4. can pay   **8.** can't OR cannot get
5. can pay

5

I've been sick for the past two days. That's why I missed the last test. May I taking [take] a make up exam?
Yes. If you bring a doctor's note.
Could my brother comes [come] to class and take notes for me on Tuesday?
Yes, he could [can].

Do you mind ~~when~~ ^{if} he tapes the class for me?

Not at all. He's welcome to tape the class.

One last request—I know I missed some
handouts. May I have ^{please} ~~please~~ ^{OR} ^{please} copies of them?

Sure. I'll give them to your brother on

Tuesday.

Thanks a lot.

UNIT 13 REQUESTS:
WILL, WOULD, COULD, CAN, WOULD YOU MIND . . . ?

❶

2. a	7. b
3. h	8. i
4. g	9. f
5. j	10. e
6. c	

Requests granted: 2, 4, 5, 6, 7, 9, 10
Requests refused: 1, 3, 8

❷

2. opening the window
3. mail a letter
4. pick up a sandwich
5. staying late tonight
6. keep the noise down
7. come to my office
8. get Frank's phone number
9. explaining this note to me
10. lend me $5.00

❸

(Note 3) Will you return please the stapler? →
Will you please return the stapler? OR
Will you return the stapler, please?
(Note 5) Would you mind leave → Would you
mind leaving
(Note 6) Could you please remember to lock the
door. → Could you please remember to
lock the door?
(Note 7) Would you please to call Ms. Rivera
before the end of the day? → Would you
please call Ms. Rivera before the end of
the day? OR Would you call Ms. Rivera
before the end of the day, please?
(Note 8) Also, would you mind to e-mail Lisa
Barker a copy? → Also, would you mind
e-mailing Lisa Barker a copy?

❹

(Answers will vary.)

UNIT 14 ADVICE:
SHOULD, OUGHT TO, HAD BETTER

❶

3. What should I wear?
4. Should I bring a gift?
5. No, you shouldn't.
6. Should I bring something to eat or drink?
7. You should bring something to drink.
8. When should I respond?
9. You should respond by May 15.
10. Should I call Aunt Rosa?
11. No, you shouldn't.
12. Who(m) should I call?
13. You should leave a message at 555-3234.

❷

2. You'd better tell
3. You'd better not leave
4. You'd better not arrive
5. You'd better write
6. You'd better dress
7. You'd better not chew
8. You'd better not call
9. You'd better not stare
10. You'd better not ask
11. You'd better thank
12. You'd better go
13. You'd better have

❸

2. you should OR ought to OR 'd better wear
3. Should I tell
4. You'd better OR ought to OR should wait
5. Should I offer
6. They should OR ought to pay OR You shouldn't pay
7. Should I write
8. should I send
9. You should OR ought to OR 'd better wait
10. I'd better not forget
11. Should I call
12. You'd better call

❹

Congratulations on your graduation! Your aunt
and I are very proud of you.

I hear you are looking for a job. You know you
really ~~oughta~~ ^{ought to OR should} speak to your cousin Mike. He's had
a lot of experience in this area. You shouldn't
~~taking~~ ^{take} the first job they offer you. ~~You've~~ ^{You'd} better
give yourself a lot of time to find something you'll

enjoy. It's important to be happy with what you do.

Maybe you should speak to a job counselor. In any case, you ~~oughtn't~~ shouldn't rush into anything! Should I ask Mike to call you? He really should ~~gets~~ get in touch with you about this.

Well, that's enough advice for one letter.

(Answers will vary.)

UNIT 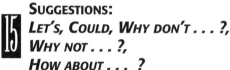 SUGGESTIONS:
LET'S, COULD, WHY DON'T . . . ?,
WHY NOT . . . ?,
HOW ABOUT . . . ?

❶

2. a.
3. b.
4. g.
5. j.
6. e.
7. i.
8. f.
9. d.
10. h.

❷

2. Maybe you could .
3. Let's .
4. How about ?
5. Why don't you ?
6. Let's .
7. Maybe we could .
8. Why don't you ?
9. How about ?
10. That's a good idea .

❸

2. take the "T"
3. go to Haymarket
4. taking an elevator to the top of the John Hancock Observatory
5. take a boat excursion
6. going to the New England Aquarium
7. eat at Legal Seafoods
8. walk along the waterfront
9. going shopping in Downtown Crossing
10. walk the Freedom Trail

(Answers will vary.)

PART PRESENT PERFECT

UNIT PRESENT PERFECT:
SINCE AND *FOR*

❶

2. looked
3. come
4. brought
5. played
6. had
7. gotten
8. fallen
9. watched
10. lost
11. won
12. eaten

❷

Since: 4:00 P.M., Monday, yesterday, she was a child

For: a day, an hour, a long time, ten years, many months

❸

Biography 1
2. since
3. Since
4. has gone on
5. For
6. have seen
7. Since
8. has earned
9. (has) broken

Biography 2
1. has been
2. for
3. has appeared
4. since
5. Since
6. has received
7. has directed
8. has formed
9. Since
10. has taken on

❹

2. **A:** How long has he been a professional golfer?
   B: (He's been a professional golfer) since he was sixteen. OR for _____ years.
3. **A:** Has he won any major tournaments since he turned professional?
   B: Yes, he has.
4. **A:** How long has he been on TV commercials?
   B: (He has been on TV commercials) for the past few years.
5. **A:** How long has Jodie Foster been an actress?
   B: (She has been an actress) for most of her life.

6. **A:** Has she won any Oscars since 1985?
   B: Yes, she has.
7. **A:** Has she directed any movies since she graduated from Yale?
   B: Yes, she has.
8. **A:** How long has she been a mother?
   B: She has been a mother since (July, 20) 1998 OR for _____ years.

5

3. Min Ho has won three awards
4. Marilyn has appeared in two movies
5. Victor and Marilyn haven't seen each other since 1998.
6. Andreas has lost three games
7. Tanya and Boris have been skaters since 1998.

UNIT **PRESENT PERFECT:**
ALREADY AND YET

1

2. acted	8. danced
3. given	9. fought
4. kept	10. known
5. held	11. drunk
6. traveled	12. smiled
7. sung	

2

1. haven't had, yet
2. 've already gotten, haven't decided yet
3. Have . . . eaten yet, 've already had

3

3. Has she gone food shopping yet? She's already gone food shopping.
4. Has she given the patient medication yet? She's already given the patient medication.
5. Has she called the doctor for the blood-test results yet? She hasn't called the doctor for the blood-test results yet. OR She hasn't yet called the doctor for the blood-test results.
6. Has she changed the patient's bandages yet? She's already changed the patient's bandages.
7. Has she given the patient a bath yet? She hasn't given the patient a bath yet. OR She hasn't yet given the patient a bath.
8. Has she taken the patient's temperature yet? She's already taken the patient's temperature.
9. Has she done the laundry yet? She hasn't done the laundry yet. OR She hasn't yet done the laundry.
10. Has she exercised the patient's legs yet? She hasn't exercised the patient's legs yet. OR She hasn't yet exercised the patient's legs.

4

It's 8:00 p.m. and I'm exhausted. I'm at my new
                    worked
job. I've already work̶ here for two weeks. The job
                                       has
is hard, but I feel that the patient h̶a̶v̶e̶ already
                                         yet
made progress. She hasn't walked a̶l̶r̶e̶a̶d̶y̶, but
she's already sat up by herself. She can feed
                             already
herself now, too. A̶l̶r̶e̶a̶d̶y̶ she has gained three
                  OR already
pounds.
    How are you? When are you coming to visit?
           decided
Have you d̶e̶c̶i̶d̶e̶ yet? Please write.

UNIT **PRESENT PERFECT:**
INDEFINITE PAST

1

2. begun	8. heard
3. forgiven	9. seen
4. promised	10. decided
5. gone	11. kept
6. felt	12. acted
7. grown	

2

2. has acted	6. have . . . felt
3. have seen	7. has kept
4. have begun	8. has promised
5. have heard	

3

2. has chosen
3. have come
4. have been
5. have not been
6. has . . . been
7. has worked
8. have . . . read
9. have rejected
10. have gone
11. have . . . felt
12. have gotten
13. have not
14. have . . . told
15. have played
16. has produced
17. have . . . been
18. have . . . seen

2. How many nominations for Best Actor have you received?
3. Have you ever seen your own films?
4. Have you ever gone to the Academy Awards?
5. How many foreign films have you acted in? OR How many times have you acted in foreign films?
6. Have you ever worked with Sophia Loren?
7. Have you (ever) been in a French film?
8. How has it changed your life?
9. Have you read any good scripts lately?

UNIT 19 PRESENT PERFECT AND SIMPLE PAST TENSE

2. Joe had
3. Joe got
4. Joe has made
5. Joe has been
6. Joe looked
7. Joe bought
8. Joe has paid
9. Joe has read
10. Joe felt

2

2. got
3. 've been
4. did . . . have
5. became
6. had
7. were
8. did . . . last
9. divorced
10. Did . . . have
11. didn't
12. 've remained
13. saw
14. have become
15. Has . . . remarried
16. hasn't
17. did . . . fail
18. got
19. didn't know
20. did . . . meet
21. were
22. did . . . move
23. 've lived

3

2. began
3. got
4. had
5. was
6. has risen
7. occurred
8. has created
9. began
10. had
11. were
12. has . . . increased
13. stayed
14. got
15. has changed
16. has reached

Last month, I have met the most wonderful guy. His name is Roger, and he is a student in my night class. He 's lived here since 1992. Before that he lived in Detroit too, so we have a lot in

common. Roger was married for five years but got divorced last April.

Roger and I have spent a lot of time together. Last week I saw him every night, and this week we've already gotten together three times after class. Monday night we saw a great movie. Have you seen The Purple Room? It's playing at all the theaters.

We 've decided to take a trip back to Detroit in the summer. Maybe we can get together? It would be great to see you again. Please let me know if you'll be there.

P.S. I'm enclosing a photo of Roger that I took a few weeks ago.

UNIT 20 PRESENT PERFECT PROGRESSIVE

2. Amanda has been working at the *Daily News* since 1999 OR for _____ years.
3. She has been writing a series about the homeless for a month OR since last month.
4. The number of homeless Americans has been increasing since 1980 OR for _____ years.
5. Pete has been working at a homeless shelter for a month OR since last month.
6. He has been studying economics for a year OR since last year.
7. Amanda and Pete have been looking for a new apartment for two months.

2. hasn't been sleeping
3. hasn't been eating
4. 's been studying
5. hasn't been working
6. 's been raining
7. 's been running
8. hasn't been waiting
9. 've been trying
10. haven't been feeling

(Answers will vary.)

2. How long has the police officer been standing
3. How long has the woman been walking
4. How long have the children been playing with the
5. How long has . . . been raining
6. How long have the men been waiting for

UNIT **21** PRESENT PERFECT AND PRESENT PERFECT PROGRESSIVE

2. has been selling	**7.** has been traveling
3. has been fighting	**8.** has received
4. have opened	**9.** has started
5. has . . . done	**10.** has written
6. has been appearing	**11.** has . . . combined

2

2. have . . . been
3. have . . . been doing
4. 've been reading
5. Have . . . read
6. 've seen
7. Have . . . bought
8. 've been using
9. has . . . opened
10. 've been opening

3

2. How much money has her business made this year?

3. How long has she been traveling around the world?
4. How many countries has she visited?
5. How many copies of her book has she sold?
6. Has she written any books since *Body and Soul*?
7. Has she ever appeared on TV?
8. How long have she and her husband lived in England? OR How long have she and her husband been living in England?

It's the second week of the fall semester. I've **been taking** ~~taken~~ a business course with Professor McCarthy. For the past two weeks we've **been** studying people who have ~~been~~ **become** ~~becoming~~ very successful in the world of business. As part of the course, we've been reading books by or about internationally famous businesspeople. For example, I've just **finished** ~~been finishing~~ a book by Bill Gates, the CEO of Microsoft, called Business @ The Speed of Thought. It was fascinating. Since then **I've been reading** ~~I've read~~ Body and Soul by Anita Roddick, the owner of The Body Shop. I've only **read** ~~been reading~~ about fifty pages of the book so far, but it seems interesting. Although I **'ve been buying** OR **'ve bought** ~~bought~~ her products ever since one of her stores opened in my neighborhood, I really didn't know much about her.

TEST: UNITS 1–8

PART ONE

DIRECTIONS: Circle the letter of the correct answer to complete each sentence.

Example:

Jackie never _____ coffee. A (B) C D

   (A) drink   (C) is drinking
   (B) drinks   (D) was drinking

1. At the moment, Meng _____ on a report. A B C D

   (A) doesn't work   (C) work
   (B) is working   (D) works

2. Water _____ at 100°C. A B C D

   (A) boil   (C) boils
   (B) boiling   (D) is boiling

3. What _____ these days? A B C D

   (A) are you doing   (C) you are doing
   (B) do you do   (D) you do

4. Do you have any aspirin? George _____ a headache. A B C D

   (A) are having   (C) have
   (B) has   (D) is having

5. Alicia _____ to the park every day. A B C D

   (A) does   (C) goes
   (B) go   (D) is going

6. When you get to the corner, _____ left. A B C D

   (A) is turning   (C) turning
   (B) turn   (D) turns

7. Walk! _____ run! A B C D

   (A) Don't   (C) Not
   (B) No   (D) You don't

8. Jennifer never _____ in the ocean.   A B C D

    (A) is swimming   (C) swimming

    (B) swim   (D) swims

9. A: Do you like spaghetti?   A B C D

    B: Yes, I _____.

    (A) am   (C) don't

    (B) do   (D) like

10. Roger _____ me at 9:00 last night.   A B C D

    (A) called   (C) is calling

    (B) calls   (D) was calling

11. There _____ a lot of people in the park yesterday.   A B C D

    (A) are   (C) was

    (B) is   (D) were

12. One day last March, I _____ a very strange letter.   A B C D

    (A) did get   (C) used to get

    (B) got   (D) was getting

13. Where _____ to school?   A B C D

    (A) did you go   (C) you go

    (B) you did go   (D) you went

14. Claude didn't _____ in Canada.   A B C D

    (A) lived   (C) used to live

    (B) use to live   (D) used to living

15. Rick left class early because he _____ a headache.   A B C D

    (A) had   (C) used to have

    (B) have   (D) was having

16. _____ is your English teacher?   A B C D

    (A) Who   (C) Whose

    (B) Whom   (D) Why

17. Who _____ yesterday at the store?   A B C D

    (A) did you see   (C) you saw

    (B) did you use to see (D) you were seeing

18. As soon as the light turned red, she _____ the car.   A B C D

    (A) did stop   (C) stops

    (B) stopped   (D) was stopping

19. They _____ when the phone rang.   A B C D

    (A) sleep   (C) was sleeping

    (B) slept   (D) were sleeping

20. Johnny _____ the paper when I interrupted him. **A B C D**
  (A) read   (C) was reading
  (B) reads   (D) were reading

21. A: Who _____ there? **A B C D**
  B: Mr. Jackson saw me.
  (A) did you see   (C) you saw
  (B) saw you   (D) you see

22. A: Whose teacher _____? **A B C D**
  B: I called Jack's teacher.
  (A) called you   (C) you called
  (B) did you call   (D) were calling

23. It _____ tomorrow. **A B C D**
  (A) rains   (C) 's going to rain
  (B) rained   (D) 's raining

24. Don't eat so much. You _____ sick later. **A B C D**
  (A) 're feeling   (C) felt
  (B) feel   (D) 'll feel

25. The package will _____ tomorrow. **A B C D**
  (A) arrive   (C) arriving
  (B) arrives   (D) be going to arrive

26. What _____ you do next month when you finish this **A B C D**
  course?
  (A) are   (C) do
  (B) did   (D) will

27. Goodnight. I _____ tomorrow. **A B C D**
  (A) 'll see you   (C) 'm seeing you
  (B) 'm going to see you   (D) see

28. Mike and I _____ to the Crash concert. We already have **A B C D**
  our tickets.
  (A) are going   (C) went
  (B) go   (D) will go

29. What will Michiko do when she _____ her license? **A B C D**
  (A) gets   (C) is going to get
  (B) is getting   (D) will get

30. That driver _____ a speeding ticket. The police are right **A B C D**
  behind him.
  (A) gets   (C) is going to get
  (B) is getting   (D) will get

31. The car of the future _____ on electricity.   A B C D
    (A) is running   (C) runs
    (B) ran   (D) will run

32. According to this schedule, the next train _____ in ten   A B C D
    minutes.
    (A) leave   (C) left
    (B) leaves   (D) leaving

33. **A:** Will you be home tomorrow night?   A B C D
    B: No, _____.
    (A) I don't   (C) I will
    (B) I'm not   (D) I won't

34. I'll see you _____.   A B C D
    (A) at the moment   (C) last night
    (B) in an hour   (D) usually

35. **A:** Why did you borrow those chairs from Jimmy?   A B C D
    B: I _____ a party next Saturday night.
    (A) had   (C) 'm going to have
    (B) have   (D) 'll have

36. **A:** Call me when you get home.   A B C D
    B: Don't worry. I _____.
    (A) don't forget   (C) 'm not forgetting
    (B) forget   (D) won't forget

PART TWO

*DIRECTIONS: Each sentence has four underlined words or phrases. The
four underlined parts of the sentence are marked A, B, C, and D. Circle
the letter of the <u>one</u> underlined word or phrase that is NOT CORRECT.*

Example:

Ana <u>rarely</u> <u>is drinking</u> coffee, but <u>this morning</u> she <u>is having</u> a cup.   A (B) C D
     A   B   C   D

37. Terry <u>usually</u> <u>drives</u> to work, but <u>today</u> she <u>takes</u> the train.   A B C D
          A   B   C   D

38. Carlos <u>usually</u> doesn't <u>eat</u> pizza, but <u>at</u> the moment he   A B C D
             A   B   C
    <u>is wanting</u> a slice.
     D

39. Frank <u>rarely</u> <u>goes</u> downtown because he <u>doesn't</u> <u>likes</u> the   A B C D
         A   B   C   D
    crowded streets.

40. Ana <u>usually</u> <u>is eating</u> in the cafeteria, but <u>these days</u> she <u>is eating</u>
       A   B   C   D
in the park.   **A   B   C   D**

41. <u>What</u> <u>you are</u> <u>studying</u> these days <u>at school</u>?   **A   B   C   D**
     A   B   C   D

42. Jackie <u>don't speak</u> French, but <u>she's</u> <u>studying</u> Spanish at the   **A   B   C   D**
         A   B   C   D
Adult Center.

43. Julie <u>loves</u> tennis, but <u>rarely she</u> <u>plays</u> because she <u>doesn't have</u> time.   **A   B   C   D**
          A   B   C   D

44. <u>Stand</u> up straight, <u>breathe</u> deeply, <u>hold</u> your head up, and <u>no look</u>   **A   B   C   D**
      A   B   C   D
down.

45. John <u>works always</u> late and <u>is rarely</u> home before 8:00 <u>at night</u>.   **A   B   C   D**
            A   B C   D

46. I <u>know</u> you usually <u>don't wear</u> a jacket, but <u>wear</u> one today because   **A   B   C   D**
      A   B   C
it <u>is feeling</u> cold outside.
      D

47. A breeze <u>is blowing</u>, the <u>sun</u> <u>shines</u>, and the sky <u>looks</u> clear and   **A   B   C   D**
              A   B   C   D
bright.

48. Paul <u>was</u> <u>drying</u> the dishes <u>when</u> he <u>was dropping</u> the plate.   **A   B   C   D**
         A B   C   D

49. When Gloria <u>were</u> a little girl, she <u>used to</u> <u>pretend</u> that she <u>had</u> a   **A   B   C   D**
              A   B   C   D
horse.

50. What <u>did</u> you <u>used to</u> <u>do</u> when you <u>felt</u> afraid?   **A   B   C   D**
         A   B   C   D

51. <u>As soon as</u> the alarm clock <u>rang</u>, she <u>woke up</u> and <u>was getting</u> out   **A   B   C   D**
      A   B   C   D
of bed.

52. Once <u>when</u> I <u>was</u> a little boy, I <u>used to get</u> sick and <u>went</u> to the   **A   B   C   D**
          A   B   C   D
hospital.

53. Who <u>you did</u> <u>see</u> when you <u>left</u> the building <u>last night</u>?   **A   B   C   D**
        A   B   C   D

54. <u>While</u> I <u>drove</u> home, I <u>turned on</u> the car radio and <u>heard</u> the news   **A   B   C   D**
     A   B   C   D
about the accident.

55. When Marie <u>will get</u> <u>home</u>, she <u>is going to</u> <u>call</u> me.   **A   B   C   D**
              A   B   C   D

56. <u>As soon as</u> she <u>finds</u> a new <u>job</u>, she <u>tells</u> her boss.   A B C D
       A   B   C   D

57. <u>I'll make</u> some sandwiches <u>before</u> <u>I'll leave</u> for the office   A B C D
     A   B   C

<u>in the morning</u>.
     D

58. According to the weather <u>forecast</u>, it <u>going to be</u> hot and sunny   A B C D
                         A   B

<u>tomorrow</u> with a chance of a thunderstorm <u>in the afternoon</u>.
    C   D

59. The doors <u>will</u> open until the train <u>comes</u> to a <u>complete</u> <u>stop</u>.   A B C D
         A   B   C   D

60. My sister <u>is going to be</u> sixteen <u>next</u> month, and she <u>has</u> a big party   A B C D
           A   B   C   D

with all her friends.

TEST: UNITS 9–10

PART ONE

DIRECTIONS: Circle the letter of the correct answer to complete each sentence.

Example:

Jackie never _____ coffee. A (B) C D

   (A) drink   (C) is drinking
   (B) drinks   (D) was drinking

1. Karen lives by _____ but she's looking   A B C D
   for a roomate.
      (A) her   (C) himself
      (B) herself   (D) ourselves

2. People in my office exchange cards with   A B C D
   _____ during the holidays.
      (A) myself   (C) ourselves
      (B) one another   (D) themselves

3. Thanks for offering to help, but I think I can do   A B C D
   it _____.
      (A) herself   (C) itself
      (B) himself   (D) myself

4. **A:** Sara is talking to Pete.   A B C D
     B: I didn't know that they knew _____.
      (A) each other   (C) them
      (B) others   (D) themselves

5. **A:** Did you say something to me?   A B C D
     B: No, I'm just talking to _____. I do
        that sometimes when I'm cooking.
      (A) me   (C) oneself
      (B) myself   (D) you

6. **A:** Help _____.   A B C D
   B: Thanks.
   (A) me   (C) you
   (B) myself   (D) yourself

7. **A:** Where are your books?   A B C D
   B: I put _____ .
   (A) away   (C) them away
   (B) away them   (D) them off

8. It's an interesting story. Please _____.   A B C D
   (A) carry out   (C) hand in
   (B) go on   (D) write up

9. When Mei-Ling doesn't know a word, she always looks it
   _____ in the dictionary.   A B C D
   (A) at   (C) over
   (B) into   (D) up

10. Please call _____ up when you get home.   A B C D
    (A) me   (C) you
    (B) myself   (D) yourself

11. It's my own fault. That's why I'm angry at _____.   A B C D
    (A) him   (C) me
    (B) himself   (D) myself

PART TWO

DIRECTIONS: Each sentence has four underlined words or phrases. The four underlined parts of the sentence are marked A, B, C, and D. Circle the letter of the one underlined word or phrase that is NOT CORRECT.

Example:

Ana rarely is drinking coffee, but this morning she is having a cup.   A (B) C D
   A   B   C   D

12. Could we talk over it before you turn the whole idea down?   A B C D
                  A   B   C   D

13. Jake stood up and introduced himself to myself.   A B C D
        A   B   C   D

14. Marta herself call the meeting off yesterday.   A B C D
           A   B   C   D

15. Do you want to get up by yourself, or would you like me to
                       A   B

    wake up you?   A B C D
      C   D

16. Don't clean up the kitchen by itself; I'd be glad to help out.   A B C D
           A B   C   D

17. Rachel and Rick know <u>themselves</u> well because <u>they</u> <u>grew</u> <u>up</u> together.   **A   B   C   D**
                           A   B   C   D

18. Sal and Christel always <u>look over</u> <u>each other</u> homework before they   **A   B   C   D**
                                   A   B

  <u>hand</u> <u>it in</u>.
    C   D

19. Before they <u>turned</u> <u>the music</u> <u>down</u>, I couldn't hear <u>me</u> think!   **A   B   C   D**
                    A   B   C   D

20. Tom asked <u>me</u> to <u>pick</u> some stamps for <u>him</u> at the post office <u>up</u>.   **A   B   C   D**
                    A   B   C   D

TEST: UNITS 11–15

DIRECTIONS: *Circle the letter of the correct answer to complete each sentence.*

Example:

Jackie never _____ coffee.   **A (B) C D**

  (A) drink   (C) is drinking
  (B) drinks   (D) was drinking

1. **A:** Would you shut the door please?   **A B C D**
   B: _____
     (A) Certainly.   (C) Yes, I could.
     (B) No, I can't.   (D) Yes, I would.

2. Why _____ a movie tonight?   **A B C D**
     (A) about seeing   (C) not seeing
     (B) don't we see   (D) we don't see

3. Marcia can't speak German yet, but after a few   **A B C D**
   lessons she _____ speak a little.
     (A) can   (C) is able to
     (B) could   (D) will be able to

4. In 1998, Tara Lipinski _____ win the   **A B C D**
   gold medal in figure skating at the Winter
   Olympics.
     (A) can   (C) will be able to
     (B) could   (D) was able to

5. I _____ make new friends since I   **A B C D**
   moved here.
     (A) can't   (C) haven't been able to
     (B) couldn't   (D) 'm not able to

6. She _____ better not arrive late.

   (A) did
   (B) has
   (C) had
   (D) would

   A B C D

7. **A:** Do you mind if I borrow a chair?
   B: _____ Do you only need one?

   (A) I'm sorry.
   (B) Not at all.
   (C) Yes, I do.
   (D) Yes, I would.

   A B C D

8. Would you mind _____ me tomorrow?

   (A) call
   (B) calling
   (C) to call
   (D) if you call

   A B C D

9. You _____ miss the deadline or you'll have to pay a late fee.

   (A) better not
   (B) 'd better
   (C) 'd better not
   (D) had no better

   A B C D

10. _____ take the train instead of the bus? It's faster.

    (A) How about
    (B) Let's
    (C) Why don't
    (D) Why not

    A B C D

11. May my sister _____ to class with me tomorrow?

    (A) come
    (B) comes
    (C) coming
    (D) to come

    A B C D

12. **A:** Would you please explain that again?
    B: Yes, _____.

    (A) certainly
    (B) I would
    (C) Not at all
    (D) I do

    A B C D

PART TWO

DIRECTIONS: Each sentence has four underlined words or phrases. The four underlined parts of the sentence are marked A, B, C, and D. Circle the letter of the <u>one</u> underlined word or phrase that is NOT CORRECT.

Example:

Ana <u>rarely</u> <u>is drinking</u> coffee, but <u>this morning</u> she <u>is having</u> a cup.
    A   B   C   D

A (B) C D

13. When <u>you will</u> <u>be</u> <u>able to</u> <u>tell</u> me your decision?
           A   B   C   D

    A B C D

14. <u>Why don't</u> <u>we</u> <u>see</u> a movie Friday night<u>.</u>
    A   B   C   D

    A B C D

15. <u>Do</u> you <u>mind</u> <u>when</u> I postpone our Wednesday <u>appointment?</u>
    A   B   C   D

    A B C D

16. <u>May</u> <u>he</u> <u>has</u> until <u>tomorrow</u> to hand in his paper?
    A B C   D

    A B C D

17. <u>Let's</u> <u>to leave</u> the party <u>early enough</u> <u>to catch</u> the last bus.   **A B C D**
    A   B   C   D

18. <u>Could</u> you <u>remember</u> <u>to bring</u> home <u>please</u> the newspaper?   **A B C D**
    A   B   C   D

19. You really ought <u>be</u> <u>more</u> <u>careful</u> or you <u>'ll get</u> into trouble.   **A B C D**
            A   B   C   D

20. <u>Would</u> you mind <u>to tell</u> me when you <u>are going to</u> <u>be</u> late?   **A B C D**
     A   B   C   D

TEST: UNITS 16–21

DIRECTIONS: Circle the letter of the correct answer to complete each sentence.

Example:

Jackie never _____ coffee.   A Ⓑ C D
- (A) drink
- (B) drinks
- (C) is drinking
- (D) was drinking

1. Anita _____ in Texas since 1991.   A B C D
   - (A) is living
   - (B) has lived
   - (C) have lived
   - (D) lived

2. John has already _____ this course.   A B C D
   - (A) been taking
   - (B) taken
   - (C) takes
   - (D) took

3. The journalist hasn't finished the article _____.   A B C D
   - (A) already
   - (B) now
   - (C) then
   - (D) yet

4. The department store has been in business _____ many years.   A B C D
   - (A) already
   - (B) for
   - (C) in
   - (D) since

5. How many cups of coffee have you _____ this morning?   A B C D
   - (A) been drinking
   - (B) drank
   - (C) drink
   - (D) drunk

6. Sheila _____ New Mexico six years ago.   A B C D
   - (A) has been leaving
   - (B) has left
   - (C) left
   - (D) used to leave

7. They have been _____ lunch in the
     same cafeteria for ten years.   **A   B   C   D**

     (A) ate   (C) eaten
     (B) eat   (D) eating

8. The Jordans _____ at R & J Corp. since 1992.   **A   B   C   D**

     (A) are working   (C) have been working
     (B) has been working   (D) worked

9. Have you read any good books _____?   **A   B   C   D**

     (A) already   (C) lately
     (B) ever   (D) now

10. It's _____ all day.   **A   B   C   D**

     (A) is raining   (C) has rained
     (B) has been raining   (D) rained

11. A: Has the mail come yet?   **A   B   C   D**
     B: Yes, it _____.

     (A) did   (C) have
     (B) has   (D) is

12. I'm sorry I'm late. How long _____?   **A   B   C   D**

     (A) did you wait   (C) have you waited
     (B) have you been waiting   (D) you have been waiting

13. A: What are you doing?   **A   B   C   D**
     B: I _____ on this report all morning.

     (A) 'm working   (C) 've worked
     (B) 've been working   (D) worked

14. _____ you cut your hair lately?   **A   B   C   D**

     (A) Are   (C) Has
     (B) Did   (D) Have

PART TWO

*DIRECTIONS: Each sentence has four underlined words or phrases.
The four underlined parts of the sentence are marked A, B, C, and D.
Circle the letter of the* <u>one</u> *underlined word or phrase that is NOT
CORRECT.*

Example:

Ana <u>rarely</u> <u>is drinking</u> coffee, but <u>this morning</u> she <u>is having</u> a cup.   **A (B) C   D**
         A   B   C   D

15. <u>When</u> she <u>was</u> a child, she <u>has worked</u> in a factory <u>for</u> more than   **A   B   C   D**
     A   B   C   D
     three years.

16. Erik <u>have</u> <u>been sleeping</u> <u>for</u> more than <u>three hours</u>.   **A B C D**
  A   B   C   D

17. Last night we <u>have rented</u> two <u>videos</u> and <u>watched</u> them with some   **A B C D**
                  A   B   C

friends.
  D

18. Jack <u>hasn't</u> <u>done</u> a thing <u>since</u> he <u>has gotten</u> to work.   **A B C D**
        A   B   C   D

19. <u>Since</u> I <u>have known</u> Tommy, he <u>had</u> three different <u>jobs</u>.   **A B C D**
      A   B   C   D

20. She <u>hasn't</u> <u>washed</u> the dishes or <u>made</u> the beds <u>already</u>.   **A B C D**
        A   B   C   D

ANSWER KEY FOR TESTS

Note: Correct responses for Part Two questions appear in parentheses ( ).

ANSWER KEY FOR TEST:
UNITS 1–8

PART ONE

1. B	10. A	19. D	28. A
2. C	11. D	20. C	29. A
3. A	12. B	21. B	30. C
4. B	13. A	22. B	31. D
5. C	14. B	23. C	32. B
6. B	15. A	24. D	33. D
7. A	16. A	25. A	34. B
8. D	17. A	26. D	35. C
9. B	18. B	27. A	36. D

PART TWO

37. D (is taking OR is going to take)
38. D (wants)
39. D (like)
40. B (eats)
41. B (are you)
42. A (doesn't)
43. B (she rarely)
44. D (don't look)
45. A (always works)
46. D (feels)
47. C (is shining)
48. D (dropped)
49. A (was)
50. B (use to)
51. D (got)
52. C (got)
53. A (did you)
54. B (was driving)
55. A (gets)
56. D (will tell OR is going to tell)
57. C (I leave)
58. B (is going to be)
59. A (won't)
60. D (is going to have OR is having)

ANSWER KEY FOR TEST:
UNITS 9–10

PART ONE

1. B	4. A	7. C	10. A
2. B	5. B	8. B	11. D
3. D	6. D	9. D	

PART TWO

12. A (it over)
13. D (me)
14. B (called)
15. D (you up)
16. C (yourself OR yourselves)
17. A (each other OR one another)
18. B (each other's)
19. D (myself)
20. D (pick up OR pick some stamps up)

ANSWER KEY FOR TEST:
UNITS 11–15

PART ONE

1. A	4. D	7. B	10. B
2. B	5. C	8. B	11. A
3. D	6. C	9. C	12. A

PART TWO

13. A (will you)
14. D (?)
15. C (if)
16. C (have)
17. B (leave)
18. D (*please* goes after *you, remember,* or *newspaper*)
19. A (to be)
20. B (telling)

ANSWER KEY FOR TEST:
UNITS 16–21

PART ONE

1. B	5. D	9. C	13. B
2. B	6. C	10. D	14. D
3. D	7. D	11. B	
4. B	8. C	12. B	

PART TWO

15. C (worked)	18. D (got)
16. A (has)	19. C (has had)
17. A (rented)	20. D (yet)